PAGAN ANARCHISM

CHRISTOPHER SCOTT THOMPSON

The following sponsors helped make this book happen:

Andrew O Forest
Judith
Christopher Angelo
Mary Lynne Biener
Kleitian

Along with the artistic and technical help of:

Ex Voto Fecit
Li Pallas
Cat Mead
Niki Whiting
Rhyd Wildermuth

PRAYER TO OUR LADY OF ANARCHY

A poem inspired by Ex-Voto's "Madonna dell'Anarchia"

Oh black-robed lady with the bleeding eyes,
Red-belted, standing on an open book,
With hands outstretched but empty. Hear our cries!
In dread and sorrow for the things you've seen
You weep for us. And yet your heart is fire.
Oh red and black Madonna, let desire
Come blazing through us till we cannot sleep.
Destroy our apathy
And help us keep
Our covenant with rage,
Our own bright fire.
And let our eyes bleed with the same desire
Until the day arrives when we shall see
Fulfillment of the prophecy
That someday soon, a flood
Shall cleanse these streets and wash your cheeks of blood.

Gods&Radicals

For inquiries, please contact us at

Editor@godsandradicals.org

or visit

GodsAndRadicals.org

WITHIN

ONE
WHAT IS PAGAN ANARCHISM?

THE black flag of anarchy is a mythic image, a magic symbol of something alluring yet threatening – much like the black cat of the witch. Like any other magic symbol, it calls up different things for different people. The idea of not being governed is intoxicating, a sip of Dionysian liberation. Yet violent chaos is terrifying, and most political philosophers ever since Hobbes have been telling us that we cannot have anarchy without violent chaos. If we accept this claim, then we must see the anarchist as a figure of mindless destruction, half-fearful and half-ridiculous. This is exactly how the State would prefer us to see the anarchist – as a cartoon image, to be laughed at or locked up as required by circumstances.

Pagans and witches face similar stereotypes. Portrayed either as laughable attention-seekers or evil servants of the powers of darkness, modern Pagans too often seek refuge in the respectability of mainstream society. This respectability is out of reach. To a society divided between atheists and religious fundamentalists, Paganism can only appear either silly or sinister.

Without respectability, outside the mainstream, Paganism and witchcraft have more to offer. In ancient times, kings and emperors were terrified of the powers of witchcraft. Instead of constantly insisting that we are not a threat, perhaps we ought to become a threat – not to human beings, but to the systems of domination and extraction that currently threaten all life on earth.

THE IDEA

In Spain before the Civil War, anarchism was known as "the Idea," and anarchist activists had a reputation for almost monastic austerity and self-discipline. Despite these semi-religious overtones, the majority of them were atheists: many were militantly hostile to organized religion. Today's anarchist movement still includes many atheists, but also a large minority of religious people—including Pagans. Pagan anarchism is a reality, a fact which might have surprised many of the past adherents of "the Idea."

So what exactly is Pagan anarchism?

Paganism and anarchism are both hard to define, because so many people attach so many different meanings to both words. To understand how these two ideas can work together, we first have to understand what they each mean separately.

PAGANISM

Paganism can mean a lot of different things. Many who use the word now refer to one particular type of Pagan religion loosely based on Wicca, often unaware that Pagan and Wiccan are not synonyms. There are many types of Paganism with little similarity to Wicca.

Scholars often use the word Pagan to refer to the polytheistic religions of pre-Christian Europe, some of which were fully organized religions with State support. Many modern Pagans also use this definition, looking to ancient forms of polytheism for inspiration and attempt to reconstruct these ancient practices.

I'm using the word in a broader sense, to refer to folk religious and magical practices focused on nature spirits, fairies, the dead and the gods. Paganism in this broader sense did not end with the Christian conversion, because it was never limited to "organized religion" in the first place. Common people all over Europe continued to leave offerings for the fairies and the dead many centuries after their official conversion to Christianity. They didn't think of themselves as Pagans in any formal sense, but continued to see the world around them filled with spirits and their daily spiritual practices reflected this worldview. They still believed in local fairy queens and fairy kings, entities that would have been understood as gods before the Christian conversion. They also retained a semi-polytheistic worldview in the veneration of saints, many of whom were not officially recognized by the church and some of whom were originally pre-Christian gods.

Peasants resisting feudalism sometimes turned to this tradition of magic and spirit worship for aid against their oppressors. For instance, Emma Wilby's *The Visions of Isobel Gowdie* documents how folk beliefs about fairy kings and the malevolent dead were used by magic practitioners in 17th century Scotland to curse feudal landowners. During the time of the Enclosures, rebels in Ireland described themselves as followers of the fairy queen Sadhbh, angered by the loss of the Commons. Similar accounts abound from other areas, showing that folk magical and religious practices were not merely "the opium of the people," but could be invoked to inspire struggles against oppression.

So when I talk about Paganism, I'm not necessarily talking about Wicca. Nor am I referring to a meticulous reconstruction of pre-Christian polytheism. Instead, I mean the religious and magical practices of the *common people*—centered on fairy spirits, the dead and other entities such as saints or gods. These practices existed alongside organized religion yet distinct from it, before the Christian conversion and after. People cultivated relationships with the spirits of nature, the dead and other entities for help with their practical daily problems—including how to effectively resist oppression.

When you combine this type of religious practice with anarchism, you get Pagan anarchism. So what is anarchism?

ANARCHISM

Most people interpret the word anarchy to mean "a society without a government." Though an anarchist society would not have a government as we now conceive of it, that isn't the origin of the word. The word comes from the Greek prefix an- or "without" and *arkhos* or "ruler." In other words, *no bosses*. This is a more useful way to understand the word, because it helps us clarify what anarchy is and what it isn't.

> **A fractured society of armed bands loyal to local warlords is not a society with no bosses— it's a society with far too many of them!**

When we think of the word anarchy as meaning "no bosses," it's clear that many of the ideas people refer to as types of anarchism really shouldn't be described that way. If you want to live in a Mad Max world of warlords and warriors, you are not an anarchist. A fractured society of armed bands loyal to local warlords is not a society with no bosses—it's a society with far too many of them! An anarchist society would reject the rule of petty local tyrants.

If you want to live in a world where anyone can do whatever they want at any time—even if that means hurting or violating other people—you are not an anarchist. A society where bullies are allowed free reign is not a society with no bosses—it's a society where any sociopath can become your boss by simply overpowering you. An anarchist society would aggressively reject all forms of domination and mistreatment.

If you want to live in a world where business is totally unregulated because there is no government, you are not an anarchist. A society with a "free market" but no government is not a society with no bosses—it's a society where your boss is all-powerful and there's nothing you can do about it: your only options are to obey or starve. An anarchist society would reject capitalism.

So there are not as many different types of anarchism as there might seem to be. There are various political philosophies that are opposed to the State, but not necessarily to other types of domination and oppression—so-called national anarchism, anarcho-capitalism and so forth. None of these philosophies are forms of anarchism, because none of them actually aim to get rid of bosses.

There are also varieties of anarchism that critique anarchist thought from one perspective or another, such as anarcha-feminism or queer anarchism. These movements don't reject core anarchist values the way anarcho-capitalism does. Instead they call other anarchists to fully examine the implications of those values.

Finally, there is also a strong tradition of individualist anarchism. This is often more a difference of emphasis than a core disagreement. All anarchist philosophies aim to give individuals the greatest possible range of personal freedom. However, not everyone values freedom highly enough to respect the freedom of others. When other people won't respect your autonomy, you can stand up to them on your own if you're strong enough —but there's no way you can always be strong enough. The only way you can ever be secure in your autonomy is to actively protect the autonomy of others. Passively respecting their autonomy (as in Right Libertarianism) is not enough, because it still leaves them without your direct assistance against bullies and predators. It also leaves you without theirs.

If you want autonomy, you must have solidarity. The only way for people to successfully resist the tyranny of would-be warlords, sociopathic predators and capitalist exploiters is to stand together, on the principle that "an injury to one is an injury to all." That means that anarchism is logically a form of communism.

Some anarchists use the word anarcho-communism. This sounds like it must describe a particular sect within anarchism, but in my opinion it really just clarifies what the word anarchism logically implies.

If some people have more than they need while others struggle, then the people who have more than they need will become the bosses. If you want to create a society with no bosses, you have to get rid of economic inequality—and that means getting rid of private property and restoring the Commons.

This might sound threatening, but "private property" doesn't refer to things you personally use, such as your clothes or your living space. Anarchists usually refer to these things as "personal property" and use the phrase "private property" for everything extra. Capitalism depends on the idea that you can own things without using them except to make money from them. That's why a single person can own a hundred houses or a dozen factories. That's why some people are homeless and most people have to work for wages. In a society without bosses, personal property would not be a problem, but private property would not exist at all. The society simply would not recognize the concept.

> **Capitalism depends on the idea that you can own things without using them except to make money from them. That's why a single person can own a hundred houses or a dozen factories. That's why some people are homeless and most people have to work for wages.**

A society with no bosses would still need a way to get things done. When no one has the power to tell everyone else what to do, you would need to get together and talk it out. You can talk until you all agree on a course of action, in which case you have consensus. Or you can agree that you'll talk for a while, take a vote and then abide voluntarily by the results of the vote. A society with no bosses would have to be directly democratic.

There's no way to run a directly democratic society on a massive scale, so a society without bosses would have to be decentralized. However, there's also no way for tiny communities like that to be completely independent, so they would have to work with other such communities. Thus, an anarchist society would be a federation of directly democratic peoples' assemblies with no concept of private property. This is the society described by most of the major anarchist thinkers, although the details vary.

So much for theory. For whatever reason, anarchists have developed an unfortunate reputation for sectarian dogmatism. If you look up "anarchism" online, you will find many densely-argued debates about the tiniest points of anarchist doctrine. This is somewhat ridiculous—in a society with no bosses, how can there possibly be one perfect system?

I believe that anarchism should be broadly understood in the terms given here, but that any sort of preset anarchist dogma is a contradiction in terms.

We shouldn't think of anarchism as a doctrine or a system, but as a critique of all existing systems. Anarchism is an approach to political philosophy in which you take a critical stance toward all claims of authority, and advocate for decentralization, equality, autonomy, and communal decision-making. It can never become a finished project; the revolution must be perpetual.

Because human beings have an instinctive capacity for mutual aid, it is not necessary to convert everyone to anarchism. In the right circumstances, people will embrace communal structures of mutual aid and decision-making whether they think of themselves as anarchists or not. For example, the vast majority of the people involved in the Occupy movement would not have identified as anarchists, but Occupy still used an anarchist model of decision-making. The role of the anarchist is to critique authority and promote autonomy and solidarity, but not to try to lead anyone to anything.

PAGAN ANARCHISM

Defining Paganism and anarchism as I have done here, how do the two ideas work together?

It all comes down to animism. If you've never interacted with spirits and you perceive the world in purely mechanical terms, you may see spirit practices as a form of superstition and an aid to various forms of oppression, while those who interact with spirits and perceive the world as being filled with them include them in their relationships—just as they might with human beings or animals.

Pagan practices are simply ways of interacting with the spirits all around us, ways of being in relationship with them. This has political implications. For instance, if the world is a dead and mechanical place, then you can blow up a mountain to get the coal inside it without worrying about anything other than practical implications. If the mountain is seen as a living thing, imbued with spirit, and a home to a number of other spirits, then you can't just do that. You have to respect the autonomy of the spirit world along with the human world. You have to stand in solidarity to resist and defeat anyone trying to commit the crime of blowing up the mountain.

If a river is just a body of water, you can dump poison in it without worrying about anything other than whether you might need to drink that water later. It's a different matter entirely if you think of it as poisoning a goddess.

If the world is just a rock we happen to live on, we can use and exploit anything we find on that rock until there's nothing else to use up. Of course, we'd die then—but it's always easy to forget about tomorrow and think only about today. If the world is alive and filled with spirit, treating everything as an exploitable object starts to look like the greatest crime in all of history.

Although the majority of modern Pagans are not anti-capitalists, there is a fundamental contradiction between the Pagan and capitalist worldviews. The worldview of capitalism is sociopathic—it treats everything and everyone as an object to be used. The worldview of Paganism is relational —not only does it not treat people or animals as mere objects, it doesn't look at anything else as a mere object either.

Earlier forms of anarchism were atheist because organized religion was a force of oppression. People are going to go on having spiritual experiences anyway, so perhaps the answer is not to deny those experiences but to acknowledge and celebrate them. If organized religion is the opium of the people, magical religion can be our medicine—healing us and giving us the strength to fight for a better world.

THE WALLBREAKER CHARM

A spell for breaking barriers and enclosures

Wild powers of the earth and air,
High walls have risen everywhere
And where we once in common held
The woods and fields, now trees are felled
To fence us in on every side
And satisfy the greed and pride
Of those who buy and sell it all.
But something doesn't love a wall...

Power of earth, cast down these stones
And shatter them like splintered bones.
Power of air, come blow them down
Until they're broken on the ground.
Power of fire, burn out these walls
Until the structure sags and falls.
Power of water, rage and flood
And sweep away these walls with mud.
Power of ice, build up so thick
You bend and buckle every brick.
Power of lightning, fast and just,
Blast walls apart and leave them dust!

Not merely walls of wood and stone
That close us in. Not walls alone,
But all enclosures you can find
Of wood or plastic, word or mind
Intended to enclose or fence
Our open space. In recompense,
Oh earth and wind and fire and flood,
I offer you, not smoke and blood,
But something dear to gods and men -
The chance to be yourselves again.

TWO
A SHORT HISTORY
OF PAGANISM

ACCORDING to folklorist Ronald Hutton, the ancient Pagan religions of the British Isles can be summed up in seven key features:

1- The worship of many different gods and goddesses, including local deities of place such as the goddess of a particular hill, gods of natural phenomena like the sun, and deities of cultural concepts such as victory or justice.
2- Communal feasts including sacrificial offerings. People ate most of the meat themselves and only dedicated a portion of the offering exclusively to the gods.
3- A festival calendar. For example, the four Irish "fire festivals" of Samhain, Imbolc, Beltane, and Lunasa—although the festival calendar was different from region to region.
4- The idea that moving sunwise (or as we would now say, clockwise) is auspicious and that doing the opposite is inauspicious.
5- Some form of existence after death. This included the belief in an otherworld inhabited by the spirits of the dead, as well as beliefs about ghosts and revenants. Some ancient Pagans believed in reincarnation.
6- Ritual deposition of valuable objects in rivers, lakes, or prehistoric burial mounds. These objects were often deliberately broken first, implying that they had to be rendered useless in our own world to be useful in the otherworld.

7- The direct worship of natural elements such as mountaintops, rivers, and springs.

Hutton wrote about the British Isles specifically, but much of this would apply to any area of ancient Europe, especially if we expressed it as a shorter and simpler list: **polytheism**, **communal feasting on holy days**, **reverence for the dead**, and **animism**. I would also add that ancient Pagans had a nearly universal belief in the power of magic and witchcraft. However, people who practiced witchcraft would have been viewed with suspicion and sometimes fear, because witches were believed to be able to curse people, wither crops, and make livestock barren.

Ancient Pagan religion wasn't focused on salvation or enlightenment but on creating and maintaining mutually beneficial relationships between humans and the spirit world.

You can see this in all of the items on Hutton's list. The worship of multiple deities includes the idea that the worshiper can obtain the help of the deities for worldly ends, as shown by the many dedications thanking a deity for help with healing or other problems. The practice of leaving offerings for the deities is closely connected to this concept, as offerings are one way to build and maintain a good relationship with the gods. Calendar festivals often marked important points in the yearly herding or agricultural cycles and were often intended to ensure good crops and healthy herds. Moving sunwise is intended to provide protection from malevolent spirits and witchcraft, while moving against the sun was believed to call up spirits and cast curses on one's enemies. Life after death implies the existence of ghosts, as well as the ability to communicate with spirits and receive counsel and guidance from ancestors. Offerings of objects in nature and the worship of natural phenomena both relate to animism, the belief that the natural world is filled with spiritual powers.

In fact, the world of spirits and the natural environment can hardly be distinguished from each other in an animist context. It's easy to see why Pagan religion appeals to people who crave a closer connection to nature and think of our modern civilization as both alienated and alienating.

FOLK RELIGION

When Christianity came, it declared the worship of multiple deities and natural phenomena to be idolatry. This created a strong trend toward alienation and away from connection, but the trend took many centuries to fully develop. Earlier scholars on this topic assumed that Pagan religions survived underground through much of the medieval period, but contemporary scholars do not support this.

With the exception of a few areas such as the Baltics, medieval Europeans would not have identified themselves as Pagans and would not have thought of their traditional practices and spirit-beliefs as Pagan religious practices. However, they still retained many of the elements from Hutton's list in modified form:

1- Polytheism was replaced with veneration of the saints. In some cases (such as St. Brigit) these saints were originally Pagan deities. Saints offered healing and protection, patronizing places and professions just like the old gods did. Many local saints were not formally recognized by the Church.

2- People still held communal feasts, including animal masking and ritual dances.

3- People still celebrated many of the same holy days as their Pagan ancestors (including the four Celtic fire festivals) as well as many new holy days dedicated to saints or events in the life of Christ.

4- Beliefs about sunwise movement continued unchanged.

5- People still believed in revenants and the spirits of the dead. In some areas (such as Bretagne) this was a major focus of folk belief.

6- People still left offerings at fountains and wells, often to request healing from a saint.

7- People still believed in a wide range of spirit beings, including fairies, trolls, elves, goblins and so on. The basic animism of Pagan religion continued, and people still tried to maintain a good relationship with the spirit world by leaving offerings and observing ritual prohibitions.

The belief in witchcraft also continued unchanged, along with the existence of healers and magicians known as cunning folk, fairy doctors, or any number of other local terms. Cunning folk were not usually seen as witches, but as specialists in dealing with the spirit world—including protection from witchcraft.

The mistake earlier scholars made was to assume that all of these practices amounted to a self-conscious attempt to preserve Pagan religion in secrecy, and that every folk custom must have an ancient pre-Christian origin. This would imply that the Christianity of medieval Europe was insincere, which does not seem to have been the case. Medieval Europe was intensely and emotionally Christian.

The reason so many Pagan elements survived for so long was subtler than that. The goals of Christianity aim beyond this world, but people still have to live in this world and solve their problems here. To survive, medieval people still needed to maintain a complex web of relationships with the spirit world. No Christian could pray to a Pagan deity without violating the tenets of the faith, but a saint could address all of the same problems as the deity anyway. As for practices such as animal masking and leaving a bowl of milk out for the fairies, most people probably saw no contradiction with their religious beliefs. Folk practices remained deeply animistic even while the people carrying out these practices were sincerely Christian.

From the Christian conversion until the Reformation, many folk practices remained broadly Pagan. However, the Reformation and the birth of industrial capitalism went hand in hand, with results that changed the entire world.

ENCLOSURE AND RESISTANCE

The feudal system of the Middle Ages was undeniably oppressive, yet there were surprisingly few rebellions against it. As catalogued by historian Norman Cohn in *The Pursuit of the Millennium*, most of the great medieval peasant revolts were not directed against the feudal system as such. Instead they were directed against changes to the existing system, changes that eroded the traditional rights of the peasantry.

Feudal lords did not have absolute authority over their tenants, as many people imagine. Instead, the power of the lords was limited by local customs that varied from one manor to the next, specifying what the lord could and could not expect from the peasants. When local conditions or political changes weakened the bargaining power of the peasantry, the lords would sometimes try to change these customs. That was when a peasant revolt would be likely to break out.

There is nothing to romanticize here: the lords were petty tyrants and the peasants knew it, as is clear from the slogan of many peasant revolts:

"When Adam delve and Eve span, who was then the gentleman?"

Despite the oppressive nature of the feudal system, the lords had limited power because the peasants could feed themselves. One of the customary rights of the peasantry was the common use of the land. Every village had a Commons, consisting of open fields and forest available for grazing and other purposes. Much of the village farmland was worked communally. The existence of the Commons contributed greatly to peasant self-sufficiency, which gave them the collective bargaining power to assert "the custom of the manor" against the arbitrary authority of the feudal lords.

As capitalism began to replace the feudal system in the sixteenth century, the early capitalists fenced off plots of land and declared them the "private property" of individual landowners in a process known as Enclosure. This is a vital point to understand, because Right Libertarians like to present private property as a fundamental human right and see the State as a force that unjustly interferes with this right. The historical reality is that private property was created through naked theft of the land from the many by the few, a process aided and abetted by the State. Without the Enclosure laws, private property would never have existed in the first place.

> With the death of the Commons and the birth of private property, capitalism destroyed the communal power of the peasantry.

With the death of the Commons and the birth of private property, capitalism destroyed the communal power of the peasantry. Peasants became a vast underclass of people who were no longer self-sufficient farmers as their ancestors had been for centuries. Left with no other means of survival, they had no choice but to sell their labor, forced to go wherever the work was available. The cities swelled with landless workers, desperate and starving, cut off from their roots and totally vulnerable. Those who could provide them with work became the lords of the earth, replacing the old aristocracy of land with the new ruling class of capital.

With the discovery of the so-called New World and the birth of colonialism, many of these people were easily sold on the idea of a better life where land was available to all—even if that meant taking it by force through the genocide of the native inhabitants. By the aggressive expansion of the new colonial empires, the lower classes of Europe became the settler colonists of America, Africa, Australia, and India.

The concept of "whiteness," and of race in general, was invented to facilitate this process. Most people aren't comfortable with simply killing other people, taking their land from them, or enslaving them. If they're defined as the Other first, it becomes much easier.

The settlers came from all over Europe. They were the heirs to hundreds of distinct regional and village cultures with different languages, folklore, festivals, and spirit practices. All these distinctions and identities were obliterated by Enclosure and capitalism, reduced and flattened to a common denominator. The European settlers had pale-colored skin. The people who already lived in these places did not.

The settlers did not share a common culture, but they did share a common skin color. Whiteness itself was a false identity, an artificial creation, invented solely to enforce the colonial system. Thus systematic racism and white supremacism were born.

All of these sweeping changes coincided with the Reformation, and the creation of harsh new forms of Christianity that presented hard work as a moral virtue—the Protestant work ethic, so convenient for capitalism. Not coincidentally at all, this unforgiving new type of Christianity viewed the folk religion of the lower classes as Pagan idolatry, to be destroyed by any means necessary. Paranoia about spiritual beliefs and magical practices swept through both Protestant and Catholic areas, resulting in the mass tragedy of the witchcraft trials.

All of these tragedies were interconnected on every level, as Silvia Federici shows in *Caliban and the Witch*. According to Federici, the new concept of the work ethic could not take hold as long as the European peasantry remained self-sufficient. The connection between people and the land had to be broken first, and people had to be taught to think of their bodies as mere machines to be used for work. Medieval women were prominent in a number of heretical religious movements promoting communal control of the land. Many women depended on the Commons for grazing, foraging and firewood, so they were often at the forefront of local struggles against Enclosure. Federici argues that capitalism could never have come into existence without first turning men and women against each other and bringing women firmly under control. The witch trials were a period of State terrorism, in which paranoia about the magical powers of women was used as a tool to destroy peasant solidarity and facilitate the Enclosures.

From this perspective the Reformation, the Enclosures, the witchcraft trials, and the birth of capitalism and colonialism were all parts of a single process. Just to give one example, my own Thompson ancestors were originally Scots. At the time of the Reformation they became Presbyterians, a stern Calvinist sect. Driven by the pressure of the En-

> **The witch trials were a period of State terrorism, in which paranoia about the magical powers of women was used as a tool to destroy peasant solidarity and facilitate the Enclosures.**

closures, they became settler colonists in Ireland and then in upstate New York. My direct ancestor, William Thompson, was a deacon of the church, with the responsibility for rooting out folk religious practices that still lingered even in the New World. He was instructed to ask church members whether they attended bonfires on Beltane, and to admonish them sternly if they did. His community in Salem, New York, was the site of one of

America's last witchcraft persecutions in 1777. Enclosure, colonialism, and the persecution of Pagan remnants and accused witches—all in the story of a single family. There were countless others.

Capitalism began by robbing the European peasantry of the Commons, then used the dispossessed as the shock troops of settler colonialism and imperialism, culminating in the horrors of genocide and the Transatlantic slave trade.

Yet there were those who fought back.

PAGAN RESISTANCE

In his column "The Revolt of Remembering" on The Wild Hunt, Rhyd Wildermuth presents an alternative history of European Paganism and the birth of the modern capitalist system:

> When we speak of Progress, too many think tech and tools, the artifice of creative mind meeting the urge to do less work. The shovel is not Progress, it is a tool—it made life easier, at least for those who dig. Nor is Progress the computer or the hand-phone, despite the lakes of toxic waste poisoning the earth that we might type at screens rather than scrawl upon paper...
>
> Progress is a religion, not a technology, a belief that what is now is better than what was before, that as-we-are is greater than as-we-were, a faith in a future unseen and a hatred of the sins of our Pagan ancestors. Before we were stupid and poor, violent and sickly until Progress came with its saving grace. Before we toiled and slaved in darkness, revering unseen spirits, chanting praises to idols and dancing ignorant dances in the meadows of The Commons; now we've got video games and factories and fast-food, praise be forever to the Holy Name of Progress...
>
> In fact, Progress is a Christian Narrative, and the religion of Empire. Christianity, aided by Empire, subjugated, displaced, and destroyed many of our ancestral ways. But not all, for the Empire which wielded the Cross as a cudgel against the heathen and the druid crumbled, as all Empires do. Pagan 'survivals' abound, despite our historian's trepidation at accepting the possibility that Empire might not be total...
>
> The destruction of Paganism was never complete, nor could it be as long as shrines to syncretized saints held place within the chapels, candles lit and rags still tied by holy springs and sacred wells, and standing stones still stood.
>
> The new can never replace the old, not fully, until the old is finally forgotten.
>
> And thus the religion of Progress, the faith which keeps us tied to our jobs, our consumption, our obedience to Empire, and our slavish sale of our

limited time in exchange for coin. But there was and still is a resistance to this religion, a revolt against the Landlords and Bosses, these priests who called "Progress" the theft of land, the subjugation of women, Africans, and indigenous peoples. And that resistance, that revolt? It was awfully Pagan.

Wildermuth goes on to cite a tale of resistance, beginning with the English settler Thomas Morton in colonial Massachusetts who wrote hymns to Pagan gods and held Mayday festivals with his friends among the local Indians.

From the 16th to the 18th centuries, a "Leveller" was a person who advocated for a classless society and "agrarian law" or common ownership of the land. Levellers often operated through secret societies such as the Hearts of Oak and the Whiteboys, led by mythic characters such as Captain Moonlight. In the 1760s, the Whiteboys resisted Enclosure in Ireland in the name of Sadhbh, their local fairy queen. They held courts in Queen Sadhbh's name and threatened the landlords, demanding that all social classes be "leveled" and the Commons restored to the people.

There were similar Pagan notes in the English Luddite uprisings and the Welsh Rebecca Riots, including practices such as masking and cross-dressing that were associated with the old Fire Festivals. In a number of cases, lingering spirit practices with Pagan undertones were used to inspire resistance to Enclosure, colonialism, and capitalism. The kings and queens of the fairies, once Pagan deities, now inspired the people to refuse and resist. Their revolts were defeated, and even the memory of them was almost entirely lost.

Yet the underground Pagan heritage was not totally dead, and it came back to life in the twentieth century.

THE PAGAN REVIVAL

The roots of the Pagan revival can be traced back to Romanticism, a hugely influential artistic movement of the 18th and 19th centuries. Romantic poets and painters valued intense emotional expression, the beauty and grandeur of nature, the mythology of old Europe, and an attitude of defiant individualism.

The Romanticists saw themselves as rebels, both politically and spiritually. This could take the form of either atheism or a vague tendency to identify with ancient Paganism and the worship of nature, along with a fascination for the occult and esoteric.

In the 19th century, this led to the creation of occult secret societies like the Hermetic Order of the Golden Dawn and various neo-druidic orders whose beliefs and practices were based on wild speculation about the ancient druid priesthood. This became something of a hallmark of modern Paganism, with some unfortunate results still making themselves felt today.

The Pagan revival has always been heavily influenced by current scholarship about the ancient Pagan religions. Unfortunately, the available scholarship until just a few decades ago was often speculative and not particularly rigorous. It also tended to be permeated with the racist, sexist, and colonialist assumptions of the scholars who did the research and wrote the books. Ideas deriving from questionable scholarship entered the Pagan community as a source of inspiration, but then fossilized into a new religious doctrine.

The modern Pagan revival is a complex movement, including sects with very little in common in terms of belief or practice. Modern Pagans can be polytheists, duotheists, animists, pantheists, or even atheists. Some practice magic and some don't. Some Pagans learn about the gods by analyzing every detail of ancient lore and some speak to their gods directly in ecstatic trance states. Many do both. Some are associated with right wing movements and some with the left. In the United States, the most common political stance for Pagans is probably mainstream liberalism, but those who identify as Heathens are more likely to be conservative.

Many reject the label "Pagan" while still fitting the general definition scholars use for the term. According to *New Age Religion and Western Culture* by Wouter Hanegraaff, Paganism is:

"all those modern movements which are, first, based on the conviction that what Christianity has traditionally denounced as idolatry and superstition actually represents/represented a profound and meaningful religious worldview and, secondly, that a religious practice based on this worldview can and should be revitalized in our modern world"

Out of all of these different types of revived Paganism, the most influential by far is Wicca and other forms of modern witchcraft.

WHEN I SHALL HAVE DEPARTED FROM THIS WORLD,
WHENEVER YE HAVE NEED OF ANYTHING,
ONCE IN THE MONTH, AND WHEN THE MOON IS FULL,
YE SHALL ASSEMBLE IN SOME DESERT PLACE,
OR IN A FOREST ALL TOGETHER JOIN
TO ADORE THE POTENT SPIRIT OF YOUR QUEEN,
MY MOTHER, GREAT DIANA. SHE WHO FAIN
WOULD LEARN ALL SORCERY YET HAS NOT WON
ITS DEEPEST SECRETS, THEM MY MOTHER WILL
TEACH HER, IN TRUTH ALL THINGS AS YET UNKNOWN.
AND YE SHALL ALL BE FREED FROM SLAVERY,
AND SO YE SHALL BE FREE IN EVERYTHING;
AND AS THE SIGN THAT YE ARE TRULY FREE,
YE SHALL BE NAKED IN YOUR RITES, BOTH MEN
AND WOMEN ALSO: THIS SHALL LAST UNTIL
THE LAST OF YOUR OPPRESSORS SHALL BE DEAD...
(FROM LELAND'S ARADIA)

MODERN WITCHCRAFT

In 1899, a folklorist named Charles Godfrey Leland published a book called *Aradia, or the Gospel of the Witches*. Leland claimed to have discovered this text while doing folklore research in Italy. *Aradia* presents a version of religious witchcraft that includes Pagan, radical, and Satanist elements. The Aradia of the title is the daughter of Lucifer and the Pagan goddess Diana. The character of Aradia seems to have been inspired by folklore about a nocturnal fairy queen associated with witchcraft, as Diana herself was portrayed in some of the historical witchcraft documents. In Leland's work, Aradia comes to teach the art of witchcraft to the oppressed peasantry so they can use it as a weapon against the nobility and the clergy.

The Scottish fairy queen Nicnevin was also seen as a queen of witches, and was also invoked in spells directed against the nobility by the peasantry according to *The Visions of Isobel Gowdie* by Emma Wilby. Based on this connection, there could well have been a widespread underground tradition of "resistance witchcraft" invoking local fairy queens with Pagan connections.

In her 1921 book *The Witch-Cult in Western Europe*, Margaret Murray argued that an ancient Pagan religion had survived in secrecy throughout the Middle Ages and that the people executed in the witchcraft trials were actually the priestesses and priests of this underground sect. According to Murray, the horned devil of the witch trials was really the Horned God of ancient Paganism.

Murray had to do a lot of intellectual gymnastics to come to this conclusion, and modern academics have universally rejected it—so much so that they tend to ignore the strongly Pagan character of some of the witchcraft trial evidence. Whatever medieval witchcraft really was, one thing is clear: it was not an organized underground religion as Murray thought.

The English poet Robert Graves published a book called *The White Goddess* in 1948. According to Graves, medieval Welsh bardic poetry by Taliesin and other famous bards encodes an ancient legacy of underground Pagan worship centered on a triple goddess who sometimes manifests as a trinity of Maiden, Mother, and Crone. There is basically nothing historically valid in the entire book—it goes far beyond speculation, and is really just a record of one man's personal vision. Most people who read the book at the time didn't realize that, and many took it for a work of scholarship.

In 1954, a British civil servant named Gerald Gardner published *Witchcraft Today*, the first in a series of books that mark the founding of modern Wicca. Gardner claimed to have been initiated into a surviving underground witchcraft coven in the 1930s. This coven might really have existed —there's no reason Gardner couldn't have stumbled on a group of practicing occultists who referred to themselves as witches. However, Wicca as it was developed by Gardner and his partner Doreen Valiente in the next few decades was clearly based on a combination of the theories of Leland, Murray, and Graves. The two main deities of Wicca are the Goddess and the Horned God, and Wiccans often speak of their Goddess as a trinity of Maiden, Mother, and Crone.

As Gardnerian Wicca grew and spread, other people came forward with their own claims of initiation into secret witchcraft lineages, leading to the proliferation of different traditions or sects such as Alexandrian Wicca. Most of these were similar to the Gardnerian version.

Wicca was originally highly secretive, and Wiccans did not actively seek new recruits. Initiates were oath-bound not to reveal the secrets of the religion, including the *Book of Shadows* (which contained the rituals). Not surprisingly, some initiates broke these oaths and started publishing the secrets, with the result that Wicca suddenly spread very rapidly starting in the 1970s.

People still practice the original initiatory versions of British Traditional Wicca, but there are also a lot of non-traditional Wiccan groups and individuals with no lineage back to Gerald Gardner or Alexander Sanders.

Wicca is still the largest and most popular branch of modern Paganism— so much so that even generic Pagan rituals designed to appeal to all types of Pagans are often based on a Wiccan framework and incorporate Wiccan concepts. However, there have always been non-Wiccan forms of Paganism and even non-Wiccan forms of witchcraft religion such as Dianic witchcraft, the Reclaiming Tradition, and the Feri Tradition.

Some of these other modern Pagan religions have been directly based on the work of Robert Graves, like the New Reformed Orthodox Order of the Golden Dawn. Others have been inspired by works of fiction, like the Church of All Worlds, based on Robert Heinlein's *Stranger in a Strange Land*. Many of these movements were much more influential in the 1960s than they are today, but Wicca and other forms of witchcraft still predominate.

The most influential strain of modern Paganism outside of Wicca includes Asatru and Heathenry and the various Reconstructionist faiths, which in turn spawned the modern Polytheist movement.

RECONSTRUCTIONIST PAGANISMS

Pagans are often voracious readers and autodidacts. Good information about the ancient Pagan religions of Europe was not widely available for a long time, but as academic research became easier to find, many Pagans became increasingly dissatisfied with the questionable history found in popular books about witchcraft.

This birthed a movement away from Wicca and other forms of modern witchcraft and toward reconstructed versions of Asatru and Heathenry (the worship of the Norse and Germanic gods), Hellenism (the worship of the Greek gods), Kemeticism (the worship of the Egyptian gods), Slavic and Celtic Reconstructionism, and so on. Due to the fragmentary nature of the evidence, the results are not necessarily much more historical than Wicca in many cases, but the goal is to accurately reconstruct ancient Pagan religions.

This strong emphasis on historical accuracy can become an almost Protestant emphasis on textual authority—"the Lore" is often considered infallible and sacrosanct, while personal mystical experience is derided as "Unverified Personal Gnosis" or UPG. Meanwhile, the emphasis on staying accurate to the practices of specific ancient ethnic groups sometimes leads to strange and ahistorical results.

Many Reconstructionists insist that it is always inappropriate to mix deities from different pantheons, a practice they deride as "eclecticism" despite the historical fact that this was a widespread and uncontroversial practice in ancient Paganism. To give one of many examples, there is an altar from ancient Britain to a goddess named Caelestis Brigantia—a combination of the North African goddess Tanit, the Roman goddess Juno, and the Celtic goddess Brigantia.

This focus on not mixing pantheons has developed in some cases into unfortunate fantasies of ethnic identity and racial purity. Fascists and white supremacists have found this a convenient cover for infiltration, although many Reconstructionists have also strongly resisted this tendency and pushed back hard against the racists.

Another aspect that sets Reconstructionism apart from Wicca is that many Wiccans tend to be "soft polytheists": identifying the gods of mythology with psychological archetypes or equating every goddess to a single Goddess and every god to a single God. Most Reconstructionists are "hard polytheists": they believe in the real existence of many gods with distinct identities. This aspect of modern Paganism has been developing into a distinct movement of its own, often referred to as the Polytheist movement.

THE POLYTHEIST MOVEMENT

A polytheist is a person who acknowledges the existence of many different gods; on its own, the word implies no specific theology or practice beyond that. Some polytheists are Wiccans, some are Reconstructionists or

Heathens, some don't fit neatly into any other category. The Polytheist movement is diverse, so diverse that it isn't really a movement at all. It may be more accurate to describe it as a tendency, a broad trend toward multiple gods and away from monotheist or duotheist theologies. There are people within the Polytheist movement who want to draw hard boundaries around it and impose strict definitions of their own creation, but this is often mere power-seeking.

Many polytheists are just as interested in ancient mythology and "the Lore" as any Reconstructionist, but instead of emphasizing what can be proved about ancient polytheism they prefer to make their own connections—direct experience is the key. Instead of disregarding "Unverified Personal Gnosis" they prefer to center it. Modern polytheism is highly personal.

Despite the huge diversity in modern polytheism, the movement as a whole could be described as being similar to a Hindu tradition called bhakti or "devotion." Bhakti practitioners cultivate emotional relationships with their chosen deity. For instance, a devotee of Vishnu might think of herself as Vishnu's lover, child, friend, servant, or even the deity's mother. The whole point of bhakti is to immerse yourself in the relationship, experiencing the full range of intense emotions associated with that role.

This is a type of mysticism or direct experience of the divine. Mysticism is passionate, intense, and ecstatic, which can seem strange or disturbing to people who haven't experienced a mystical encounter with a deity. Polytheists often describe themselves as the lover, "godspouse," personal friend, or even servant of the god. A few overemphasize the servant aspect, forgetting that service is only one of several possible relationships between human and deity. In bhakti traditions, service to the deity is sometimes seen as an early stage, with romantic love and equal friendship as more desirable states. From this perspective, those who emphasize blind obedience and conventional piety mistake a partial perspective for the whole.

RADICAL PAGANISM

"I have heard it said that a land wight does not care about the politics of who summons it. This is a glib statement. It is politics which enables the destruction of the very land which the wight stands guard over. Man is a political animal, those who say that they are outside of, or above, politics are the esotericists whose clean hands are washed in the blood of those who have no choice but to put their hands in the machinery. Politics is not optional for First Nations, women, queers, blacks, or any of the other slave classes. Abstention is a position of privilege which aids the pattern of

destruction, arguing only for our impotence. There is no left-right dichotomy, there are those who are destroying the body, and those who stand against them. Economics is war by other means, and in this asymmetric war against life itself, you do not have the luxury of choice. This is the time when our witchcraft again becomes an imperative, or perishes."
 Peter Grey, "Apocalyptic Witchcraft"

The Pagan revival includes the full range of political positions, including fascism and white supremacism, mainstream conservatism and liberalism, and anti-capitalist radicalism. Pagan anarchism is a subset of the Pagan Left. (So-called "National Anarchists" are also frequently Pagan, but their movement is a contradiction in terms and really just a confused branch of the fascist Right.)

Some modern Pagans claim to be staunchly apolitical, seeing radical Paganism as a highly unwelcome trend that corrupts religion by mixing it with politics. Political neutrality is conservative by default. When the entire world is under threat from industrial capitalism, what does it mean for a Pagan to be apolitical? It can only mean that you will allow mountains be blown apart for coal, forests to be clear-cut, rivers to be poisoned, and the Earth to be overheated until it becomes unlivable. From the perspective of animism, that can only mean that you are no friend to the spirits but a collaborator with those who would destroy them and leave us all with a dead world.

Pagan anarchists don't make rules for other people. No one is saying that a Pagan is "not allowed" to be a supporter of capitalism. You're always allowed to do whatever you choose—but that doesn't mean it makes sense. You can be an "apolitical Pagan" if you want, but the consequence of your apolitical position will be the death of everything you claim to worship.

Radical Paganism itself encompasses a range of positions, including not only anarchism but communism, anti-fascist and anti-racist activities, and environmental activism.

Heathens United Against Racism (or HUAR for short) works to counter the influence of racism and fascism in the Heathen movement. HUAR is well-known in the Heathen community for its strong opposition to "Folkish" Asatru based on "European blood." This stance is especially important given the involvement of some Folkish Heathens in the fascist Traditionalist Worker Party—the group whose members stabbed several anti-fascist activists in Sacramento, California, in 2016. HUAR and many other Heathen organizations subsequently signed on to a statement called Declaration 127, rejecting the Asatru Folk Assembly's racist and homophobic stance.

The Warrior's Call is a Pagan anti-fracking organization that has developed its own sigil or magic symbol for use by anti-fracking activists. Members of The Warrior's Call engage in both traditional protest activities and magic or ritual forms of protest. Some members wear the group's sigil as a tattoo, a talisman providing courage and protection during direct action.

Several well-known Pagan or occult writers are also active in radical politics. Starhawk's *Spiral Dance* was a major factor in the birth of the Goddess movement, but Starhawk also promotes eco-anarchist ideas through novels such as *The Fifth Sacred Thing*. Starhawk was also an active participant in the Occupy movement, and is a founding member of the activist Reclaiming Tradition of witchcraft.

Rhyd Wildermuth and Alley Valkyrie, the two founders of Pagan anti-capitalist website Gods & Radicals, were both well-known as radical Pagan writers before they started the website. Gods & Radicals brings together writers from a number of different perspectives and also publishes the print journal "A Beautiful Resistance," including Pagan anti-capitalist poetry and essays.

Writer and publisher Peter Grey's *Apocalyptic Witchcraft* is a manifesto of radical magic, an explicit call for the use of witchcraft as a tool of resistance. Grey defines witchcraft as "the recourse of the dispossessed, the powerless, the hungry and the abused" and declares that "If the land is poisoned then witchcraft must respond."

Many if not most Wiccans subscribe to an ethical code known as the Wiccan Rede, defined as "An it harm none, do as ye will." The Wiccan Rede is often paired with the Rule of Three, the belief that any action for good or ill will magically return to the witch threefold. Many Wiccans cite the Rede and the Rule of Three to "prove" that real witches do not work curses, as any negative magic would only rebound on the witch who used it.

Historically speaking, Grey is absolutely right—witchcraft was seen as a weapon. To be more specific, witchcraft was a weapon used by people who didn't have access to other weapons. When the emperor's troops destroy your village, you cannot strike back at him directly—so you work some magic. How many Gauls cursed Julius Caesar before the first dagger struck him? The Caesars of our own time are even more powerful and more dangerous, destroyers of entire ecosystems and wielders of weapons that can erase cities in an instant. Against such forces as these, no ancient witch would have hesitated to use all available tools. In the ongoing struggle against the power of Capital, witchcraft must reclaim its place as "the recourse of the dispossessed."

THREE
THE STORY
OF AN IDEA

ANARCHY'S history is the history of humanity. As demonstrated by James C. Scott in *The Art of Not Being Governed*, claims to authority are always resisted by someone. There have also been stateless societies that existed for centuries.

Anarchism as a political philosophy is a more recent phenomenon, an Idea we can trace through history to a handful of thinkers. And despite the traditional link between anarchism and atheism, the connections between anarchism and Paganism also go right back to its origins: the revolutions of the 18th century.

BIRTH OF THE IDEA

"Sacred Goddess, Mother Earth,
Thou from whose immortal bosom
Gods and men and beasts have birth..."

These lines are from a poem by Percy Bysshe Shelley, one of the Romantic poets whose sympathy for ancient Paganism cleared the way for the modern Pagan revival. Shelley's wife Mary was the daughter of Mary Wollstonecraft (one of the founding thinkers of modern feminism) and of William Godwin (widely considered the founder of anarchism).

Wollstonecraft and Godwin were strong defenders of the revolution in France, and active participants in the "Revolution Controversy" between British writers in the 1790s. Thomas Paine's *Rights of Man* offered early support for the French Revolution. Edmund Burke, another British writer, came out against it with an attack on Paine. Wollstonecraft replied with *A Vindication of the Rights of Men*, to be followed by *A Vindication of the Rights of Woman*, her main contribution to feminist thought.

Godwin weighed in with *An Inquiry Concerning Political Justice*. In this work, he laid out the basic principles of what we now call anarchism, though he never actually used the term. Godwin was strictly a philosophical anarchist, not a revolutionary. His respect for individual autonomy led him to reject all forms of coercion and violence, even in the name of mass liberation. Most of the anarchist thinkers since Godwin have rejected pure pacifism, but have accepted his basic idea of a decentralized and directly democratic society without a State.

Godwin's preferred political unit was based on the parish. Later anarchists would use the word "commune" for the same concept—a small community governed by all its members equally via consensus or direct democracy. In Godwin's philosophy, parishes would send delegates to work with other parishes on matters of regional concern, but these loose federations would never be allowed to fossilize into a new State. All power would flow from below rather than above. The anarchist tradition since Godwin has largely been based on the same idea.

About the same time that Godwin was proposing his ideas in England, a Scotsman named John Oswald was proposing almost exactly the same philosophy in revolutionary France. An active revolutionary (unlike Godwin), Oswald was fated to die in combat. He never attained the fame or influence of Godwin, but his proposal for a "Universal Commonwealth" of directly democratic people's assemblies is just as clearly a forerunner of later anarchist thought. Oswald was also either a Pagan or sympathetic to Paganism. His vegetarian tract *The Cry of Nature* imagines the distant past as an egalitarian animist utopia:

> But not to the animal world alone were the affections of man confined: for whether the glowing vault of heaven he surveyed, or his eyes reposed on the greeny freshness of the lawn; whether to the tinkling murmur of the brook he listened, or in pleasing melancholy melted amid the gloom of the grove, joy, rapture, veneration filled his guileless breast: his affections flowed on everything around him; his soul around every tree or shrub entwined, whether they afforded him subsistence or shade: and wherever his eyes wandered, wondering he beheld his gods, for his benefactors smiled on every side...

Pierre-Joseph Proudhon (1809-1865) was the first thinker to self-identify as an anarchist. He defined anarchy as a society without masters or sovereigns—in other words, no bosses—or as "order without power." The idea that anarchy represents not chaos, but order, is the meaning of the most widely known anarchist symbol: the A for anarchy inside an O for order.

Proudhon has left us with one of anarchism's most well-known denunciations of the evils of government:

> To be governed is to be watched over, inspected, spied on, directed, legislated at, regulated, docketed, indoctrinated, preached at, controlled, assessed, weighed, censored, ordered about, by men who have neither the right, nor the knowledge, nor the virtue to do so. To be governed is to be at every operation, at every transaction, noted, registered, enrolled, taxed, stamped, measured, numbered, assessed, licensed, authorized, admonished, forbidden, reformed, corrected, punished. It is, under the pretext of public utility, and in the name of the general interest, to be placed under contribution, trained, ransomed, exploited, monopolized, extorted, squeezed, mystified, robbed; then, at the slightest resistance, the first word of complaint, to be repressed, fined, despised, harassed, tracked, abused, clubbed, disarmed, choked, imprisoned, judged, condemned, shot, deported, sacrificed, sold, betrayed; and, to crown all, mocked, ridiculed, outraged, dishonoured. That is government; that is its justice; that is its morality.

Proudhon proposed a system based on self-governing workers' associations with no concept of private property, but retained some features of a market economy such as credit and trade. He referred to this system as Mutualism, and "mutual aid" remains a core anarchist principle. Proudhon's philosophy is often interpreted as a step toward libertarian communism or anarcho-communism, anarchist philosophy in its classic form.

While Proudhon was proposing this early version of libertarian communism, German philosopher Max Stirner (1806-1856) took the opposite approach. Stirner is usually named as a founder of individualist anarchism, due to his dismissal of the State and every other form of authority as a mere "spook" or mental construct. In Stirner's philosophy, there are no legitimate restrictions whatsoever on the human self or Ego. Unlike later egoists such as Ayn Rand, Stirner never said that people ought to act in their own self-interest, only that *they always do*, whether consciously or unconsciously. An unconscious egoist might passively submit to exploitation and abuse, due to superstitious respect for the authority of the exploiter. A conscious egoist would fight back, recognizing the abuser's authority as another "spook." Stirner advocated for a free society based on a Union of Egoists, and made it clear that he recognized no concept of private property. As such, Stirner's individualist anarchism differs from anarchist communism less than it might initially appear.

LIBERTARIAN COMMUNISM

In the United States, the word "libertarian" almost always refers to a philosophy that would more accurately be referred to as the Libertarian Right, the most extreme manifestation of which is so-called anarcho-capitalism.

In other parts of the world, the word can just as easily refer to the Libertarian Left, the anarcho-communist tradition of Mikhail Bakunin (1814-1876), Peter Kropotkin (1842-1921), and Emma Goldman (1869-1940). This version of communism is "libertarian" because it rejects the idea of creating communism through the State or of forming even a temporary communist government in order to implement the revolution.

Instead of imposing communism from above through a revolutionary vanguard, Russian anarchist Mikhail Bakunin believed that workers should seize the means of production directly and create communism from below. This would involve a General Strike to bring down the capitalist system and all its power structures. The working class would occupy shops and factories, and resume operations under worker self-management. The new society would be run by a combination of these democratic workplaces and neighborhood communes, and the revolution would be defended by armed workers' militias with elected officers.

In the historic struggle between Bakuninite anarchists and Marxist communists that split up the First International Workingmen's Association in 1872, Bakunin's supporters argued that any communist revolutionary government would not "wither away" but become a self-perpetuating tyranny. The resulting split between anarcho-communists (often called simply "anarchists" for short) and authoritarian communists (often called simply "communists") continues to this day.

Unlike Godwin or Proudhon, Bakunin was no pacifist but an active revolutionary. He participated in several uprisings, did time in prison, survived exile in Siberia, and provided the theoretical basis for anarchism's unfortunate association with terrorism in the public mind. It was Bakunin who coined the phrase "propaganda of the deed":

> In the United States, the word "libertarian" almost always refers to a philosophy that would more accurately be referred to as the Libertarian Right

(W)e must spread our principles, not with words but with deeds, for this is the most popular, the most potent, and the most irresistible form of propaganda.

Bakunin himself had moral limits, rejecting the extreme tactics of the terrorist Sergey Nechayev after working with him for some time. However, some anarchists of the following decades embraced the use of bombings and assassinations, a wave of terror attacks that resulted in the stereotype of the anarchist as a mad bomber.

Bakunin's successor Peter Kropotkin rejected terrorism, although he accepted the fact that the revolution would have to be defended by force once it occurred. Kropotkin also defended the principle of expropriation, or the direct seizure of private property without compensation during the revolution. Private property beyond what is needed for personal use is seen as theft by anarchists, so expropriation is not a form of robbery but a remedy for it.

Kropotkin's philosophy began with a critique of Social Darwinism, a white supremacist ideology that misused Charles Darwin's "survival of the fittest" as a justification for imperialism and racism. Where Darwin had emphasized the role of competition as a driving force in evolution, Kropotkin argued that cooperation and "mutual aid" had contributed just as much to the survival and development of species.

Where Darwin had emphasized the role of competition as a driving force in evolution, Kropotkin argued that cooperation and "mutual aid" had contributed just as much to the survival and development of species.

He then applied this scientific insight to political philosophy, arguing for an anarcho-communist society with no monetary system. Society would be decentralized into self-governing directly-democratic communes, and each able-bodied member of a commune would be expected to work for about four or five hours a day on some necessary task. Every member of the commune would be free to use any food or other supplies necessary for survival. Those who refused to help the community in any way could be ostracized from participation in the commune, but Kropotkin believed such people would be few.

Kropotkin's theory of cooperation, or mutual aid, became a major tenet of anarchist philosophy, inspiring Food Not Bombs, the Common Ground Collective, and Occupy Sandy. When the State fails to provide aid to those in desperate need of assistance, anarchists have repeatedly stepped forward to take up the slack.

Mutual aid is not the same thing as charity. Charity is something handed down from above and administered by professionals, often with a strong element of condescension and judgment and always with complicated layers of bureaucracy. Mutual aid is built from the ground up by ordinary people, and controlled by the community through directly-democratic procedures. In the eyes of the State, mutual aid seems to be as threatening as armed insurrection. The Common Ground Collective was by far the most effective force on the ground helping survivors of Hurricane Katrina in Louisiana, but it was infiltrated by a notorious informant for the Federal Bureau of Investigation in order to spy on the anarchists.

> **Mutual aid is built from the ground up by ordinary people, and controlled by the community through directly-democratic procedures. In the eyes of the State, mutual aid seems to be as threatening as armed insurrection.**

Mutual aid provides many of the same services as the State, but more effectively and democratically. It could be considered a "proof of concept" for the anarchist Idea. As such, the State is probably justified in considering it a serious threat. Mutual aid on a large enough scale would mean revolution.

Kropotkin lived long enough to return to Russia for the Revolution of 1917, only to be bitterly disappointed by the oppressive nature of the Bolshevik regime. Just like Bakunin, he had warned that authoritarian forms of communism would only replace one tyranny with another—and history proved him right.

Bakunin, Kropotkin and most of the other anarchists of this era were staunch atheists. However, there were already Pagans involved in the movement. George Watson MacGregor-Reid, the eccentric founder of the Ancient Druid Order, was also a militant labor organizer and an anarchist communist. Reid's druid organization eventually split into several distinct groups, including the Order of Bards, Ovates & Druids which is still the largest neo-druidic organization.

In Reid's words:

"Under a state of voluntary or Anarchist Communism the rights of the individual will be respected. The human race is entirely communistic in its tendencies, and it is the falsity of individualistic doctrines, and workings, that has brought into existence the miseries and wrongs which to-day threaten the best interests of the commonweal."

ANARCHISM IN ACTION

Godwin's philosophical and pacifistic version of anarchism was largely hypothetical, but the events of the Industrial Revolution created real misery and oppression for working people. Hypothetical concepts on their own don't liberate anyone, but they can light a spark in those who wish to liberate themselves. As the working classes built their labor movement in the 19th century, anarchism developed from an abstract philosophy into a plan of action.

THE PARIS COMMUNE

In 1871, France's defeat in the Franco-Prussian War triggered an urban uprising in Paris, in which a coalition of revolutionaries and radicalized National Guardsmen successfully took over the city and declared a revolutionary Commune. Paris was home to half a million industrial workers, and many of them were involved in radical anti-capitalist organizing. Anarchists inspired by Proudhon were one of the major factions in the Paris Commune and succeeded in introducing some anarchist elements into the Commune's policies. For instance, factories abandoned by their capitalist owners were handed over to worker control (although factories whose owners remained in place were not).

One of these anarchists was a woman named Louise Michel, a legendary militant of the Paris barricades, who was known as "The Red Virgin of Montmartre." A kind of anarchist saint, she could be seen as a living prototype for Makhno's "Mother Anarchy" and the Madonna dell'Annarchia. It was Michel who first carried the black flag as a symbol of anarchism.

The Paris Commune had anarchist features, but was timid about expropriating private property. The Commune never solidified its revolutionary gains, and was eventually crushed by the French Army in an appalling massacre known as the "Bloody Week."

ANARCHO-SYNDICALISM IN THE US AND EUROPE

On May 4, 1886, someone threw a bomb at police during a protest for the eight-hour workday at Haymarket Square in Chicago. The bomb was said to have been retaliation for recent police murders of labor protesters. In the ensuing chaos, seven police officers and four civilians were killed and there were many injuries. Eight anarchists were charged with planning the attack, but the evidence was flimsy. Four of them were hung and one committed suicide in jail to avoid execution. These men were known as the "Haymarket Martyrs," and annual marches to commemorate their fate became the modern May Day. For an anarchist Pagan, the tradition of anarchist street protests on May Day dovetails perfectly with the ancient Beltane fire festival.

Anarchist labor organizers built a powerful movement over the next few decades, producing the variety of anarchism known as anarcho-syndicalism. Syndicalist trade unions seek to replace the State with federations of directly democratic worker-managed syndicates. Spain's National Confederation of Labor or CNT (from "Confederación Nacional del Trabajo"), founded in 1910, is one such union. The Industrial Workers of the World or IWW, also known as the Wobblies, has never explicitly identified as anarcho-syndicalist but is still firmly within the same tradition.

The IWW, CNT, and allied unions waged a steady series of aggressive strikes, and took a leading role in the bloody labor struggles that won the eight-hour work day and other victories for working people. They also suffered many casualties, murdered by hired gunmen or the forces of the State. To defend against the constant violence, the CNT created a network of armed defense committees that would later become the anarchist militias of the Spanish Civil War. There were also anarchist revolutionaries outside the syndicalist movement, such as the Italian insurrectionist Errico Malatesta.

RUSSIA AND THE UKRAINE

In 1917, the fall of the Czar created an opportunity for Russian and Ukrainian anarchists. The Ukrainian anarchist organizer Marusya (Maria Nikiforova) formed a militia known as the Black Guards. This organization fought throughout the Ukraine, but also had a large contingent in Moscow as the military wing of the Moscow Federation of Anarchist Groups. In 1918, the new Bolshevik secret police force attacked and destroyed the Black Guard headquarters in Moscow—the first of many clashes to come between authoritarian and anti-authoritarian communists.

Marusya's ally, Nestor Makhno, transformed his own Black Guard unit into the Revolutionary Insurrectionary Army of Ukraine, also known as the Black Army. The Black Guards and the Black Army fought for an anarchist revolution throughout the Civil War, but were eventually outlawed by the Bolshevik authorities. Marusya was captured by White Russian forces and executed, while Makhno was forced to go into exile.

ANTI-FASCISTS

In 1919, the CNT was behind the General Strike in Barcelona, which won the eight-hour workday for Spanish workers. In the aftermath of this huge strike, employers began a reign of terror against the CNT. Hitmen called *pistoleros* assassinated many labor organizers, and the *pistoleros* of the CNT defense committees hit back as well as they could. Spain was slowly drifting toward civil war, as the country was bitterly divided between conservatives, liberals, communists, and anarchists.

In the 1920s and 1930s, fascism appeared and began to spread. Different fascist movements had different characteristics, but all of them stressed an aesthetic of militarism and brute force, including the violent rejection of democracy and egalitarianism. Despite their differences, anarchists and communists all over Europe united to fight the fascist threat. Anti-fascist streetfighters in Italy and Germany did everything they could to prevent a fascist takeover, but were ultimately unsuccessful.

However, anti-fascists helped prevent a similar tragedy in Britain. In the famous Battle of Cable Street in 1936, 100,000 anarchist, communist, and Jewish protesters crushed an attempted fascist march through

WHAT'S FASCISM?

Fascism is an authoritarian ideology that seeks to claim control of the State in order to enforce strict hierarchies upon society.

In Fascist ideology, certain people are fit to rule, while others are fit to obey. Those who don't fit into either category are fit to be destroyed.

Obedience to leaders and submission of the self to the mythic ideal of the Nation, the People, the Folk, or other totalitarian constructs is key to all Fascist movements.

Fascism sometimes (but not always) employs racism, anti-Semitism, and anti-immigrant sentiment in its goal of creating a monolithic, superior culture.

Anarchists fiercely oppose (and often wage street battles against) fascists, especially since Fascism espouses a violent, anti-egalitarian view of the world.

the East End of London. The anti-fascist slogan "They shall not pass!" is often attributed to this fight.

Anarchism was not just a European phenomenon, nor was fascism. When Japan came under the control of fascist Emperor-worshipers, the anarchists fought back. Both Korea and Manchuria were Japanese colonies at the time. In 1929, Korean anarchists established the Shinmin Autonomous Region in Manchuria, and held out against Japanese forces until 1932.

In 1936, several Spanish generals sympathetic to fascism began a rebellion against the elected government of Spain. This government was basically reformist with some communist influence, but the anarchists and communists both rallied to prevent a fascist victory. The CNT took over Barcelona, and inaugurated the longest and most successful experiment at creating an anarchist society ever seen.

For the next few years, the CNT put the anarchist Idea into action throughout the Catalonia region. Businesses were collectivized and put under worker self-management. Society was restructured around self-governing neighborhood communes. Anarchist worker militias fought the fascists at the front, while the CNT pursued the social revolution behind the lines.

Unfortunately, the CNT was persuaded to join a coalition government with the communists and liberals. This was a direct contradiction of anarchist principles, and was followed by a brutal and decisive crackdown in the name of anti-fascist unity. By the time the fascists won under General Franco, the CNT was once again an underground revolutionary organization. The first great era of militant anarchism ended in defeat.

NEW DIRECTIONS IN ANARCHISM

With the defeat of anarchism in Spain, the movement went into a steep decline. Anarchist and syndicalist organizations were subject to intense repression. From 1871 to 1939, anarchism had become an increasingly successful and militant revolutionary movement. With this movement's defeat, many surviving anarchists decided that armed struggle had been a tragic failure. They returned to the pacifism of Godwin, and dwindled into an insignificant minority in Leftist circles.

Despite this loss of influence, anarchism has been developing in interesting new directions ever since. Many of these new developments address internal hypocrisies, pointing out aspects of anarchism that had previously been self-contradictory. For instance, Proudhon was a misogynist and Bakunin was an anti-Semite. These positions are contradictory for an anarchist to hold—anarchism is by definition opposed to hierarchy, so placing men above women or one race or religion above another is inconsistent with anarchism. Modern anarchists strongly reject sexism, racism, and every other form of bigotry even if they are not always very good at recognizing racist and sexist tendencies in themselves.

ANARCHA-FEMINISM

Anarcha-feminism as a distinct movement dates back to the classic period of anarchism before the defeat in Spain. Emma Goldman and Voltairine de Cleyre, two American writers and activists, both advocated for a feminist anarchism. Goldman was the most influential American anarcho-communist during her own lifetime, and de Cleyre was an equally influential individualist anarchist. The phrase "direct action," so often heard among anarchists, is the title of an essay by de Cleyre on effective revolutionary tactics. Another anarcho-communist named Lucy Parsons was also an active feminist. Born into slavery in 1853, Parsons was one of the founding members of the IWW, and her husband was one of the Haymarket Martyrs. Parsons was such an effective revolutionary organizer that the Chicago Police Department described her as "more dangerous than a thousand rioters." During the Spanish Civil War, there was also an active anarchist women's militia called Mujeres Libres. One of the most well-known modern anarcha-feminists is the Pagan writer Starhawk, founder of the Reclaiming tradition of radical witchcraft.

POSTCOLONIAL ANARCHISM

Postcolonial anarchism combines the core ideas of classical anarchism with an anti-colonial and anti-racist analysis, including strong support for the autonomy of indigenous cultures. Post-colonial anarchists point out that there have always been cultures without the State, including tribal cultures without fixed social classes or formal rulers. Therefore, anarchy cannot be considered solely a European idea even though the classical anarchist philosophers were European. This movement is related to the APOC (Anarchist People of Color movement) and "Panther anarchism," an anarchist movement that developed among former Black Panthers such as Lorenzo Kom'boa Ervin.

QUEER ANARCHISM

Strong prejudice against homosexuality was once the norm among many leftists, including anarchists. Homosexual behavior was seen as a decadent affectation of the upper classes and therefore anathema for any serious leftist. Of course, this prejudice was nonsense, and there were always gay and bisexual people in the anarchist movement. Just to give one example, the anarchist women's militia in Spain was founded by lesbian writer Lucía Sánchez Saornil. Queer anarchism seeks to address the contradiction, arguing that anarchist principles of personal autonomy imply liberation of all aspects of life, including sexuality.

ANARCHO-PRIMITIVISM

Anarcho-primitivism rejects not only the State but civilization itself. This is a major new development in anarchist thought, and a clear departure from the tradition of libertarian communism. Primitivism is part of a broader movement known as "green anarchism," which incorporates eco-logical thinking into anarchist discourse.

American writer Murray Bookchin's philosophy of libertarian municipal-ism, in contrast with anarcho-primitivism, seeks to create an ecologically harmonious anarchist society in an urban environment.

INDIGENOUS ANARCHISM

The most interesting development in anarchism in recent years is proba-bly the unexpected rebirth of the movement and the development of new militant revolutionary groups inspired by anarchism. The Zapatistas of Mexico do not call themselves anarchists, but their philosophy of building power from below resonates with anarchist ideas. The Zapatistas were themselves the inspiration for much of the anti-globalization movement of the turn of the millennium, including the "Battle of Seattle" in which the anarchist Black Bloc succeeded in shutting down the 1999 World Trade Organization conference.

AND MORE

All over the world, new mass movements with anarchist elements have exploded since the financial collapse of 2008—including the Arab Spring, Spain's *Indignados*, the Occupy Movement, and France's *Nuit Debout*. In the Kurdish parts of Syria, an anarchist-inspired revolutionary militia has been building a society based on Bookchin's philosophy.

Anarchism seems to finally be recovering from its defeat in the 1930s, and who knows what the next hundred years will bring?

FOUR
BRINGING THE
MAGIC BACK

THE anarchism of Bakunin and Kropotkin was a product of the 19th century, an era in which most radicals were optimistic about "progress" in all its forms.

Many people in that era saw science and technology as unequivocally positive, or even as a necessary prerequisite for an anarchist society. Kropotkin was so enchanted by the possibilities of technology that he believed massive, steam-driven dishwashing machines would liberate women from the drudgery of housework, thus making anarchist society a feminist society.

A lot of things have happened since then (including dishwashers!), and it is no longer possible to view either science or technology through such rose-colored glasses. That doesn't mean we should reject them either, but we can no longer think of them as unqualified benefits. Everything from nuclear war to global warming should make that impossible for any thoughtful person.

On the other hand, the mindless rejection of scientific fact by such a large percentage of the population could well prevent us from doing anything about these problems before they destroy our civilization.

If neither religious fundamentalism nor unquestioning optimism about science is in our interest, is there a third option that might serve us better?

THE NEED FOR A NEW ANIMISM

The sociologist Max Weber, in 1917, laid out the close relationship between science, capitalism, and the end of magic:

The fate of our times is characterized by rationalization and intellectualization and, above all, by the disenchantment of the world.

According to Weber, a modern capitalist economy would be impossible in a society still dominated by magical thinking. The process of disenchantment began with Christianity, which strongly rejected all magical practices, then progressed much more rapidly under the influence of scientific agnosticism:

"*Since Judaism made Christianity possible and gave it the character of a religion essentially free from magic, it rendered an important service from the point of view of economic history. For the dominance of magic outside the sphere in which Christianity has prevailed is one of the most serious obstructions to the rationalization of economic life. Magic involves a stereotyping of technology and economic relations. When attempts were made in China to inaugurate the building of railroads and factories a conflict with geomancy ensued. The latter demanded that in the location of structures on certain mountains, forests, rivers, and cemetery hills, care should be taken in order to not disturb the rest of the spirits.*"

In other words, it wasn't possible to cover China with railroads and factories as long as the traditional magic of feng shui was still predominant. There would have been too many restrictions on where and how such things could be built. Railroads and factories may have their benefits, but if they are built everywhere with no restrictions the result is a toxic landscape with nothing living in it.

The apostles of progress tend to think of science as a force of liberation, but the history of science is much more checkered than that. As Silvia Federici says in *Caliban and the Witch*:

"*The incompatibility of magic with the capitalist work-discipline and the requirement of social control is one of the reasons why a campaign of terror was launched against it by the state—a terror applauded without reservations by many who are presently considered among the founders of scientific rationalism... Even the materialist Hobbes, while keeping his distance, gave his approval... He added that if these superstitions were eliminated, "men would be much more fitted than they are for civil obedience."*"

Whether rational or not, magical thinking prevented the unrestricted growth of industrial civilization. A disenchanted worldview removes that barrier. That's why industrial civilization has grown so rapidly and destructively under disenchanted forms of religion (such as Protestant Christianity) and disenchanted philosophies such as Soviet communism. Anarchists have always denied that the Soviet system was truly communist, referring to it as "State capitalism." From the ecological standpoint, the reason for this is obvious—authoritarian communism and capitalism are equally disastrous for the environment. They both emphasize endless growth with no restrictions.

Weber saw this "rationalization" as an economic benefit, but not necessarily a human benefit.

> "Man is dominated by the making of money, by acquisition as the ultimate purpose of his life. Economic acquisition is no longer subordinated to man as the means for the satisfaction of his material needs. This reversal of what we should call the natural relationship, so irrational from a naïve point of view, is evidently as definitely a leading principle of capitalism as it is foreign to all peoples not under capitalistic influence... No one knows who will live in this cage in the future, or whether at the end of this tremendous development entirely new prophets will arise, or there will be a great rebirth of old ideas and ideals, or, if neither, mechanized petrification, embellished with a sort of convulsive self-importance. For of the last stage of this cultural development, it might well be truly said: 'Specialists without spirit, sensualists without heart; this nullity imagines that it has attained a level of civilization never before achieved.'"

The real danger of this type of thinking is not merely that we have become a "nullity," vainly imagining our spiritually dead civilization to be superior. Rather, the true danger is in how we act now that we are no longer capable of seeing the world and everything in it as being alive. Seeing everything as a dead object, we use things up and throw them away on mountains of garbage that grow larger with every passing day. Our civilization has become a cancer, rapidly killing its host: the biosphere.

A revival of animism, a re-enchantment of the world, holds much more potential for creating an ecological society than any number of scientific papers demonstrating the reality and danger of climate change.

The only answer science can give us for this is a rational one. Scientists can and do try to save us from our destructive choices, presenting one rational argument after another. They are consistently ignored, because reason is—and always has been—a weak tool for changing human behavior. Religious thinking is much more powerful for this purpose. Unless we return to some form of animism we are probably doomed.

Primitivists would argue that technology itself is the problem. This is a debate worth having, but for the record I do not agree. Knowledge is simply knowledge—"the truth is the truth," as Max Weber said on his deathbed—

but religion can give us a context for how to use this knowledge without destroying ourselves and everything around us.

By embracing animism and treating everything as a person, we may yet have a chance. People don't treat other people particularly well, but there is at least a general acknowledgment that we ought to. A revival of animism, a re-enchantment of the world, holds much more potential for creating an ecological society than any number of scientific papers demonstrating the reality and danger of climate change.

In a straightforward sense, this it is what people experience before becoming brainwashed into ignoring what they see and feel. My four-year-old daughter frequently points out "magic trees": trees distinguished by a particularly vibrant spiritual energy. Children have to be taught not to see such things. When we tell children that "fairies aren't real" we brainwash them into our own disenchanted form of adulthood. We should instead tell them that these things are real, but they are nothing like what they might see in a Disney movie. To see a fairy in real life, look for a "magic tree." They're all around.

In the book *Original Wisdom*, Robert Wolff writes of his experiences among indigenous peoples with animist worldviews. They consistently report seeing and feeling things that we do not. The societies Wolff describes are also non-hierarchical and have a low ecological impact. In a sense, you could say that they are Pagan anarchist societies—and they work.

The most ancient way of thinking on the planet may also be the only one with any future for us.

I ARISE TODAY

In an animist view, the world we live in is alive with spiritual energy. Stones, lakes, trees, and mountains are all inhabited by spirit. The spirits in the landscape take many forms, including all of the different fairy tribes of traditional folklore. In animist practice, worship is given to natural forces and to the spirits within the landscape itself. This is even more basic than the worship of the gods.

The British writer Gildas, in the 6th century, mentioned that the Pagans in his area had worshiped the mountains, fountains, rivers, and hills. When St. Patrick was describing the God of his faith to Loegaire's daughters, they asked him whether he was talking about a sky, earth, sea, river, mountain, or valley god. Kentigern similarly complained that the Pagans of his district in Scotland worshiped "the elements."

Some of the most beautiful poems in the Gaelic oral tradition are addressed to the sun or the moon, and one is addressed to the thunder. All of these are described in the Irish lore as being *duilean* or "elements," showing that the Gaelic conception of the elements was not the same as the classical four elements system but could include any of the basic or primal forces of the natural world.

One traditional Gaelic prayer refers to the Christian God as the "Lord of the Elements." Others invoke the power of the elements for healing and protection:

Power of storm be thine,
Power of moon be thine,
Power of sun.

Power of sea be thine,
Power of land be thine,
Power of heaven.

Power of wind I have over it,
Power of wrath I have over it,
Power of fire I have over it,
Power of thunder I have over it,
Power of lightning I have over it,
Power of storms I have over it,
Power of moon I have over it,
Power of sun I have over it,
Power of stars I have over it,
Power of firmament I have over it,
Power of the heavens
And of the worlds I have over it,
Power of the heavens
And of the worlds I have over it.

Another prayer to the elements can be found in the famous poem attributed to St. Patrick, known as "The Deer's Cry." Most scholars don't believe he actually wrote it and this verse doesn't mention anything specific to Christianity. I suspect it was originally a popular prayer or charm, borrowed from the oral tradition and incorporated into the longer, Christian version of the Deer's Cry:

I arise today, through
The strength of heaven,
The light of the sun,
The radiance of the moon,
The splendor of fire,

The speed of lightning,
The swiftness of wind,
The depth of the sea,
The stability of the earth,
The firmness of rock.

In the Irish legends, the gods themselves swear oaths by the elements and expect the elements to hold them to those oaths, so one could argue that the basic forces of the natural world are the gods of the gods, a primal animism underlying the polytheism of Irish mythology.

ANIMIST PRACTICE

Gildas also mentions that the Pagans he was familiar with worshiped fountains. Taking a pilgrimage to a holy well is an ancient pre-Christian custom, although many of the holy wells still existing in Europe are now dedicated to Catholic saints. In Ireland, people seeking relief from some affliction will travel to renowned holy wells to drink their water, often after "circumambulating" or walking around the well clockwise a number of times while reciting prayers in silence. There is often a rag tree or clootie tree beside the well, where pilgrims can tie a little piece of cloth in hopes of leaving their illness behind.

There is spiritual symbolism in both the silence and the clockwise walking. Many traditional healing practices are only valid when conducted in total silence, and some require a period of total silence while coming and going as well. The clockwise walk represents the movement of the sun across the heavens. If you stand facing east, you will see the sun rise in front of you, move to the south, and then set in the west over the course of a day.

Walking sunwise is an effective counter against the attentions of hostile spirits; walking against the sun can call them up according to some traditions. Slow, thoughtful sunwise walking in total silence is an excellent spiritual practice, a form of walking meditation. Combining this practice with prayer is even better. You can say the prayers beneath your breath to maintain your silence if you prefer. Here is one prayer I use myself:

To the shining moon above us
And the gentle sun that loves us,
To the stars that pierce the sky.

To the bright green trees that feed us
And the rich warm earth beneath us,
To the darkness and the light.

To the oceans that surround us,
Deep abysses dark and boundless:
Come and walk with me tonight.

OFFERINGS AND INCENSE

Like many other Pagans, I often leave offerings as a way to build and maintain a good relationship with the spirits. I'll prepare a dish of food and pour a drink, then leave them both on my altar beside a burning candle or stick of incense.

I never eat this offering myself. According to the tradition I practice, the spirits consume all the goodness of the offering and what is left over is no longer food. When I leave an offering outdoors, it is sometimes eaten by birds or animals. That's not a problem, as I would simply think of them as stand-ins for the spirits.

In many traditions, there are different offerings for different types of spirit. For instance, when I want to make an offering to the underworld spirits, I will usually pour a libation into a hole in the earth so that it trickles down underground. To make an offering to the land spirits, I would leave a bowl of milk, a piece of cheese, or some other small treat outdoors. To make an offering to the celestial spirits, I would burn a stick of incense or a small piece of food to send the smoke and the odor of the food up to the heavens.

On occasion, Pagans in North America have received warnings from Native acquaintances that offerings of alcohol should never be poured directly into the ground, as they will attract the attention of malevolent spirits. If you live in North America and are concerned about this possibility, you can simply use blessed water or milk instead of alcohol.

If you're trying to establish an animist practice, the most important thing is just to listen to your own feelings. The sunwise walking, prayers to the elements, and leaving of offerings are all ways to reconnect, to re-enchant your own experience of the world by getting to know the spirits all around you. When you feel one of these spirits reach out to you, don't second-guess it. Listening closely to subtle feelings is the antidote to alienation.

TO THE GOD
OF THE WOOD

Will you meet me in the thick wood where the shadows shine and the sunlight falls so thin it leaves no record on the wind?

Will you walk in the tall trees where the whispers walk, where I've heard you wail?

Will the fury of a sudden breeze make your name a crazy call?

In groves where light can never reach will you become the sound of birds?

And when my silence is my speech, will you remove my need for words?

God of the woods, with the laughing eyes, you are a world of pale stars in a purple sky beneath the wildness of the night.

You are the tears of the dead bards who whispered sadly when you smiled; you are my years of wasted words—so come and walk with me awhile.

Dark-haired, bright-eyed, drunken god, your hard face, your beastlike walk—our world has grown to need your grace. It is no longer time for talk.

Though in your eyes there is no time, or world, or sight, but only space; though hints of holy rage and crime distort the joy that lights your face,

Yet hearts are known by what they love and peoples by the creed they serve—and this time more than any time should have the god that it deserves.

FIVE

BONFIRES AND REVELRY: PAGAN PRIMITIVISM

I FIRST became a Pagan around age 12, when I was living in a tent in the woods along a dirt road in Maine. My family was building a stack-wall log cabin, where we would live for about four years as homesteaders. We had no electricity or running water, no indoor plumbing, and no telephone. I carved a figure out of wood, brought it to my father and asked him if we could put in the vegetable garden to placate the spirits there. That may have been my first conscious act of Pagan religious practice.

Critiques of modern civilization are usually met with derision and ridicule. Who would want to give up all our modern conveniences? It's a fantastic daydream, and would be a horrible experience in real life—or so they tell themselves. I've actually lived that way, so I know they're wrong. It's a lot easier to live without modern technology than you would ever think.

Many Pagan anarchists identify with anarcho-primitivism or "anti-civ," a branch of anarchist thought that sees the primary cause of oppression as civilization itself. Some anarcho-primitivists see the problem as being agriculture, and seek to create a new society inspired by the freedom and low ecological impact of hunter-gatherer societies.

Anarcho-primitivism is starkly different from classical anarchism because it aims to resist all forms of industrial civilization. Classical anarchist thinkers such as Kropotkin were not opposed to industrial technology, only to the misuse of that technology to control and exploit people. Although anarcho-primitivists are anti-capitalist, they would also be opposed to an industrialized anarchist society. According to A *Primitivist Primer* by John Moore:

"For anarcho-primitivists, civilization is the overarching context within which the multiplicity of power relations develop... Civilization - also referred to as the megamachine or Leviathan - becomes a huge machine which gains its own momentum and becomes beyond the control of even its supposed rulers. Powered by the routines of daily life which are defined and managed by internalized patterns of obedience, people become slaves to the machine, the system of civilization itself."

In place of the traditional anarchist commune or people's assembly, anarcho-primitivists prefer the band—in anthropological terms, a family-based group of between five and eighty people. It's easy to see how a band could be run according to anarchist principles, with shared rituals and spirit practices of a Pagan character. A band would live much closer to nature than most humans now do, and would more easily develop a spiritual relationship with the hills and forests, the streams and ponds. The appeal of primitivism to Pagan anarchists is not hard to understand. However, not all anarcho-primitivists are sympathetic to Paganism.

One essay, "To Rust Metallic Gods," subtitled "An Anarcho-Primitivist Critique of Paganism," takes the entire Pagan revival to task for idealizing Europe's polytheistic past. According to this essay, all of the Pagan religions of Europe enshrine a patriarchal mentality of violence and subjugation. The symbolism of our most ancient myths reflects the adoption of agriculture, and the alienation of humankind from nature. According to the author:

"So what then of the historical Pagan societies? As clerical religions, they atrophied participatory spiritualities rooted in place. Increased human domination of landscapes coincided with personification of natural forces as humanoid figures, with distancing from primeval elements and phenomena. These militaristic chiefdoms and kingdoms may have claimed to worship the land, but they owned the land as property. They mined the land for copper and tin and iron. The initial transition from gathering surface clay or salt or flint to gathering surface copper or tin or bog iron may have occurred gradually, but the additive consequences reveal an extractive orientation. They had class hierarchy, slavery, and conquest. Anti-authoritarians have no good reason to venerate or romanticize 'heathen' conquerors."

As the author points out, the veneration of war gods and conquerors seems more appropriate for fascism, and modern European fascist movements have appropriated Pagan myths and symbols. Many people involved in Paganism express semi-fascistic ideas about warrior honor and the sacred nature of hierarchy. These ideas are obviously totally inappropriate for an anarchist form of spirituality, so the author encourages Pagans to turn away from ancient gods and myths and embrace a new animism:

> "...worship of sun, fire, and moon directly. Appreciation for lunar and solar cycles. Solstice and equinox celebrations. Reverence for rivers, forests, marshes, hills. Altars and shrines for local spirits. Feasts, bonfires, and revelry."

That all sounds wonderful, and I would argue that any Pagan revival lacking an animist component would not be truly Pagan. Yet to those of us who see the gods (in our dreams or otherwise), they cannot simply be ignored. We love what we love, and devotional polytheism is a relationship of love. When I light a candle and pray to Brighid, I see the flame—but I also see the goddess and feel my heart well up with love for her. That's just a fact, whether anyone else approves of it or not.

The author also neglects the fact that war gods can be invoked by either side of a conflict. In the *Second Battle of Moytura*, the three war goddesses known collectively as the Morrígan fight in the rebellion of the gods against the tyrannical Fomorians. A myth can be interpreted in more than one way, and I see no reason a modern polytheist could not pray to the Morrígan before engaging in acts of resistance against the State.

In modern Hong Kong, the war god Guan Di receives prayers from Triad gangsters, the police who hunt those gangsters, and the protesters of the Umbrella Revolution movement. As Heathen Chinese wrote in the essay "Are The Gods On Our Side?" on Gods & Radicals:

> "It seems reasonable to conclude that Guan Di has, at times, answered the prayers of both sides of a conflict simultaneously. It seems further reasonable to extend this pattern to the ongoing conflict that some call 'the class war.' Guan Di has thousands and thousands of worshipers with whom he maintains relationship on both sides of said war."

The Guan Di who answers a protester's prayer is no more or less real than the Guan Di who answers a gangster's prayer or the prayer of a police officer. As a deity of conflict, it is simply in Guan Di's nature to answer prayers related to conflict. Heathen Chinese goes on to say:

> "As the worship of many gods is restored in the West, it is therefore the responsibility and duty of anti-capitalist/anti-racist polytheists and neo-Pagans to make their voices heard as loudly as possible. Ask for your gods' help in our collective struggles before the other side does."

So I cannot accept the rejection of Pagan religion by some anarcho-primitivists. What about their opposition to civilization?

CHRISTOPHER SCOTT THOMPSON

EMPIRES CRUMBLE

Most people lacking a clear understanding of anarchism would define "anarchy" as violent chaos, or what happens when central government collapses. In 1991, Somalia collapsed into a patchwork of warring factions when the dictator Siad Barre was overthrown. Few people would argue that the average Somali person was better off during the civil war than under Siad Barre. Being ruled by a tyrant is not a good thing, but having to deal with a different tyrant in every neighborhood is even worse.

It must have been similar when the last Western Roman emperor was deposed in 476, or when the Ashikaga shoguns lost control of Kyoto in 1467.

> "Now the city that you know
> Has become an empty moor
> From which the skylark rises
> While your tears fall."

These are the words of a samurai official (as translated by historian Stephen Turnbull) after the beautiful temples and feudal palaces of ancient Kyoto had been destroyed by civil war. The Ashikaga shogunate had lost its power, its claim to hold a monopoly on the use of force. The result was horrifying, a breakdown of social order throughout the entire nation of Japan. For a hundred years, samurai warlords known as daimyo waged petty local wars with each other for the control of territory. The "Age of Warring States" was a century-long bloodbath, ending only when a series of tyrants succeeded in crushing all opposing clans and uniting Japan under a new shogun.

The men who united Japan were no better than those they conquered. Oda Nobunaga, for instance, marched into battle under a banner reading "Rule the Empire Through Force." His samurai set fire to a Buddhist holy mountain outside of Kyoto and then marched up the hillside, methodically cutting down any monks who came running in panic out of the burning temples. Yet despite their brutality, the conquerors justified their actions because their conquests put a stop to war. When the Tokugawa clan came out on top, Japan remained at peace for more than 250 years.

The distinction between the Age of Warring States and the so-called Pax Tokugawa is what most people think of as the difference between anarchy and civilization. When civilization breaks down—as in the reduction of Kyoto to an "empty moor" during the Onin War—humanity fractures into senseless violence. Gang bosses war with each other over local power, and ordinary people are left with nothing. Only a strongman can restore society, a tyrant capable of controlling all lesser tyrants and establishing a new monopoly on the use of violence.

This monopoly on the use of violence is what we call the State, and people tolerate it or even celebrate it because they think it brings peace. Certainly the "Age of Warring States" was not a peaceful time, but was the Pax Tokugawa truly peaceful?

BEHIND THE MASK

During the years of Tokugawa rule, there were more than 5,400 peasant uprisings in Japan. Many of these local rebellions sought a reduction in the crushing taxes imposed by feudal lords. The peasants often won the initial skirmishes against their samurai rulers, but in the end the authorities were always able to crush these rebellions because they had access to firearms and the peasants did not. In some cases, peasants who could not or would not pay their taxes were wrapped in bales of straw and burned alive. Rebels were crucified along the sides of the road. Very often, the local lord would then agree to lower the taxes and meet the demands of the peasants—but only after crushing the rebellion first. The peace of the Tokugawa was only an illusion, maintained through both the threat and the reality of horrific violence.

Chaos and violence or a violent order, but never peace and freedom for the common people: this is the reality of all forms of Empire, including those from our Pagan past. The religion of the Roman Empire was a broad-minded polytheism, but the Pax Romana was a peace of terror. In words attributed to the Scottish chieftain Calgacus, the Roman historian Tacitus gives us an eloquent account of what any empire really is:

"They plunder, they butcher, they ravish, and call it by the lying name of 'empire.' They make a desert and call it 'peace.'"

The Roman Empire was one of the world's great civilizations, and is still idolized by many Pagans as a time when polytheism thrived throughout Europe. Yet this is what one of its greatest writers had to say about it at the height of its power. When civilizations are built with the blood of the conquered, the only people impressed by them will be those who benefit— or those so far removed from the reality of the situation that they cannot smell the blood or hear the screams.

The same applies to modern Liberal Democracies. People suffer and die every day so we can live our lives the way we do. The oceans rise, the cities swelter, species disappear from the planet at a dizzying pace. Our world is changing, becoming less hospitable to life. For as long as we can, we will go on pretending that nothing is really wrong, or that the problems can be fixed with a few cosmetic reforms. We are killing our own species, and we're so unwilling to stop doing it that most of the debate is about whether we should do "too little, too late" or do nothing at all.

Even for Pagans who reject primitivism, the anarcho-primitivist critique has relevance. The world is obviously in crisis, and the crisis could well be terminal. We could be approaching a future in which the Earth is no longer livable, or will only support a much smaller population. Perhaps the only way to preserve this planet as a living biosphere is to destroy the source of the crisis: our technological society.

"BY ANY MEANS NECESSARY"

This is the perspective of Deep Green Resistance, a controversial anti-civ organization. According to their *Statement of Principles*:

> *"Civilization, especially industrial civilization, is fundamentally destructive to life on earth. Our task is to create a life-centered resistance movement that will dismantle industrial civilization by any means necessary."*

This sounds apocalyptic, and raises the possibility that millions of people would have to die before the primitivist society could come into being. According to Derrick Jensen of Deep Green Resistance:

> *"The grim reality is that both energy descent and biotic collapse will be ever more severe the more the dominant culture continues to destroy the basis for life on this planet. And yet some people will say that those who propose dismantling civilization are, in fact, suggesting genocide on a mass scale... Polar bears and coho salmon would disagree. Traditional indigenous peoples would disagree. The humans who inherit what is left of this world when the dominant culture finally comes down would disagree."*

This uncompromising position appeals to some, but it is clearly a picture of mass destruction even if only to prevent a greater harm. The controversy surrounding Deep Green Resistance is partly inspired by this extreme position, but also by their virulent rejection of transgendered people.

We can argue theory all we want, but theory has something inhuman about it. It's all abstract; it's based on chains of logic alienated from life. My attitude to this question is not abstract or theoretical. When Deep Green Resistance attacks transgendered people, they are attacking people I personally know and love. I reject that absolutely, and there is no room in my mind for compromise.

Deep Green Resistance has also made it clear that anyone unable to survive without modern medical technology would have to be allowed to die. According to Derrick Jensen:

"I have Crohn's disease, and I am reliant for my life on high tech medicines. Without these medicines, I will die. But my individual life is not what matters. The survival of the planet is more important than the life of any single human being, including my own."

It's obviously true that the life of the planet is more important than any individual life, but Deep Green Resistance is talking about a future in which we allow millions of people to die because they aren't physically perfect enough to survive without modern technology. An organization that holds these positions can be nothing but anathema to me.

So we'll leave that aspect of the controversy to the side, and concentrate on the anti-civ question. In my opinion, a strong case can be made that industrial civilization is irredeemable. It's hard to imagine a society based on any lifestyle similar to that of the modern United States that would not be destructive to all life on Earth. Everything about the way we live demands a global economy of extraction and exploitation—one that must double in size every twenty years to maintain corporate profits and avoid collapse. According to an article in The Guardian by Jason Hickel:

"Let's imagine, just for argument's sake, that we are able to get off fossil fuels and switch to 100% clean energy. There is no question this would be a vital step in the right direction, but even this best-case scenario wouldn't be enough to avert climate catastrophe... When it comes to climate change, the problem is not just the type of energy we are using, it's what we're doing with it. What would we do with 100% clean energy? Exactly what we are doing with fossil fuels: raze more forests, build more meat farms, expand industrial agriculture, produce more cement, and fill more landfill sites, all of which will pump deadly amounts of greenhouse gas into the air. We will do these things because our economic system demands endless compound growth, and for some reason we have not thought to question this."

Green capitalism is a suicidal fantasy. If human civilization is to endure, it will have to change both quickly and drastically. That is the fundamental moral imperative behind modern revolutionary activism.

Does this mean that civilization itself is the enemy? I don't know that it does. There is no universally-accepted definition of the word "civilization," but one traditional definition is simply "urban society." The Classical Mayan civilization disappeared around 900 AD when the Mayan people abandoned the cities and returned to the countryside, where their descendants still live today. So there is precedent for the deliberate abandonment of urban civilization. That doesn't make it a viable option for us today.

If billions of people suddenly left the cities to return to nature, the ecological devastation would be incalculable. Anarcho-primitivists don't want this to happen, so it's hard to see how an anarcho-primitivist society could come into existence without mass slaughter. According to John Moore:

> "The personal view of the present writer is that population would need to be reduced, but this would occur through natural wastage - i.e., when people died, not all of them would be replaced, and thus the overall population rate would fall and eventually stabilise."

I do not find this convincing. For one thing, a significant global decline in population would prevent the doubling of the economy so necessary for capitalism, triggering a catastrophic collapse of civilization with a much more rapid population loss. Unless we've already replaced the capitalist system with something that isn't based on growth, this scenario ends up being just as destructive as any intentional mass murder. Perhaps anarcho-primitivism could only begin to develop after classical anarcho-communism takes hold, but I don't think that's what Moore was proposing.

It comes down to the individual anarcho-primitivist.

If their position is like that of Deep Green Resistance, which speaks of triggering the fall of civilization intentionally, then I don't see how anyone who values the sanctity of life can possibly support them.

If their position is simply that civilization will collapse on its own—and that the best way for the survivors to live after the fall is to adopt anarcho-primitivism—then I think they may be right. I don't intend to wait around for that to happen while there is still the smallest chance of a better outcome, and that is why I am not an anarcho-primitivist.

Historian Peter Linebaugh suggests a better way forward:

> "Since the city, in the sense of law, force, and commodity, has abolished the countryside commons and the 'bourgeois' nations destroyed the 'barbarian' ones, the commoners of the world can no longer retire to the forest or run to the hills. Unprecedented as the task may historically be, the city itself must be commonized."

For most of human history, it was surprisingly easy to escape the reach of the State. As James C. Scott shows in *The Art of Not Being Governed*, most historical States led a precarious existence. No ruler could create an empire without vast reserves of concentrated manpower, yet people could simply walk away from the State at any time and escape to the forests and hills—and they often did. The ruined cities studied by archeologists didn't necessarily fall prey to any dramatic catastrophe. In many cases, they simply couldn't continue to function because so many people chose to leave them. For many centuries, States were small islands of slavery surrounded by huge ungoverned wildernesses and the "barbarians" who lived there. Most of the world was a free Commons. Empire-building, industrialization, and capitalism have destroyed this Commons, and there is no longer anywhere left to run. With our backs to the wall, our only real option is to free the cities.

I believe that Kropotkin was right in *The Conquest of Bread*, when he argued that a future urban civilization could be based on the well-being of all rather than the profit and power of a few. Kropotkin was a product of the Industrial Revolution, so he didn't realize how destructive it would be to continue that lifestyle even under anarcho-communism. If there is ever an anarchist society based in the cities, they will have to be eco-cities or they will not endure.

If we should ever be so lucky as to see that happen, perhaps there will also be bands of anarcho-primitivists living outside the cities and close to nature, worshiping the spirits of the land with "feasts, bonfires and revelry." It sounds like a wonderful life.

MILLENNIUM

Black birds come screeching through the skies
On winds of war, as waters rise.
And prophet's eyes begin to gleam
Beneath their floating hair. This dream
Of smoke and fire shall end at last!
A whisper rises from the past—
Millennium—as pillars shake
Millennium—as gods awake
Millennium—as flowers bloom
In mouths of corpses, and the tomb
Springs open to reveal the Host
Arranged for battle, ghost by ghost,
With banners flapping, black and red.
Millennium—"We are the dead
Who rose with Spartacus and fell,
Who sang John Ball Has Rung Your Bell,
Who marched with pitchforks on Versailles,
And those who answered Boukman's cry,
Who rode with Makhno in Ukraine,
And those who died defending Spain.
We are the dead of all the earth
Who died to bring this day to birth.
The dead who dreamed another world
Have come to you with flags unfurled.
The burning wheels and turning gears
Have come around. The end is near.
Our work remains undone. But you
(Millennium!) shall see it through.
So take your mental spear, and go!
Cast down all thrones. Let forests grow
Where burning mills once filled the sky
With smoke and flame. Let empires die,
Till none is slave and none is king.
Then heal. Then build. Then sing."

SIX
IN THE NAME
OF THE UNDEAD

STRANGE dreams are stirring, drifting into the sleeping consciousness of mystics, visionaries, and revolutionaries. Dreams of the fallen and most often the forgotten—those who fought in all of the uprisings and revolutions since the beginning of history. They stir on the edges of sleep like revenants besieging a presidential palace. They want us to hear them and to heed their call.

In *The Return of the Dead: Ghosts, Ancestors, and the Transparent Veil of the Pagan Mind*, the scholar Claude Lecouteux traces the persistence of beliefs about the dead and the undead from Pagan into Christian Europe. According to our ancient Pagan ancestors, some dead people come back—often angry at those they left behind, always dangerous.

The circumstances in which a person might become a revenant are fairly clear according to Lecouteux. Essentially, a person who dies young or through violence cannot always move on, but remains in a twilight world between the dead and the living. They will often remain this way until they complete some task, finish a mission as yet undone.

What did those who fought with Spartacus leave undone? Those who marched in the name of John Ball during the English Peasant's Revolt? Those who raised the machete for Boukman in Haiti or rode with Makhno in the Ukraine?

Total liberation for everyone. This is the mission of the fallen and forgotten. In the name of the dead revolutionaries of all past generations, we must make this mission our own.

Radical Paganism is millenarian.

A THOUSAND YEARS OF ANARCHY

Sounds great, doesn't it? Actually, why not ten thousand years of anarchy? We know that bosses in some form have been around for at least that long, so it only seems fair that we should be free of them for the same amount of time! But actually, I don't mean to be taken quite so literally.

The word "millennium" means one thousand years, and entered English referring to the thousand-year reign of Christ prophesied in the Book of Revelations. Throughout the Middle Ages, peasant revolts were usually led by charismatic prophets and messiah figures, claiming that they were about to usher in the millennium by divine command. This often involved a horrible bloodbath targeting anyone the messiah didn't like—rich people, Jewish people, and anyone who didn't support the immediate ushering-in of the apocalypse.

As chronicled by Norman Cohn in *The Pursuit of the Millennium*, most of these prophets were mass murdering tyrants—not people any anarchist would want to emulate. However, not all of the medieval millenarian movements were so horrifying. The Brethren of the Free Spirit, for instance, were philosophical Christian anarchists who believed that the laws of neither Church nor State could be applied to the saved. (Cohn argues that they were also ruthless criminals, but unconvincingly.)

Scholars now use the word "millenarian" much more broadly, to refer not just to these medieval Christian movements but to any mass revolutionary movement guided by religious prophesy to bring about a total transformation of society—including the Ghost Dance religion of the 1890s, which inspired Native resistance to white settlement of the American West. Clearly, my vision of the revolutionary dead demanding that we finish their work is millenarian in this broader sense.

There were also a number of Taoist-inspired millenarian rebellions in Chinese history, and some of these were even bloodier and more destructive than those of the medieval Christian prophets. This raises a vital question: can we dream of a revolutionary transformation of society without unleashing the demons of mass destruction?

SUMMER WITHOUT FLOWERS

At the end of the *Second Battle of Moytura*, the Morrígan delivers two contradictory prophecies. One describes a future of prosperity and abundance, the other describes the downfall of the Celtic social order and the collapse of humanity's relationship with the natural world:

I shall not see a world that will be dear to me.

Summer without flowers,
Kine will be without milk,
Women without modesty,
Men without valour,
Captures without a king.

Woods without mast,
Sea without produce,

Wrong judgments of old men,
False precedents of brehons,
Every man a betrayer,
Every boy a reaver.
Son will enter his father's bed,
Father will enter his son's bed,
Everyone will be his brother's brother-in-law.

An evil time!
Son will deceive his father,
Daughter will deceive her mother.
(Trans. Elizabeth A. Gray)

No distinction is made between the Morrígan's two prophecies, implying that either or both could just as easily come to pass. However, the same pattern is repeated in the *Colloquy of the Two Sages*, and this time the happy prophecy made by the upstart bard is a sign of his relative lack of wisdom, while the terrible prophecy of Ferchertne wins the war of words between the two. Ferchertne's prophecy is too long to quote in full, but here are some relevant passages:

The cattle of the world will be barren.
Men will cast off modesty.
Every one will pass out of his (proper) state through pride and arrogance, so that neither rank nor (old) age, nor honour, nor dignity, nor art, nor instruction will be served.
Every noble will be condemned: every baseborn will be set up, so that neither God nor man will be worshipped.
Inhospitality will destroy flowers.
Through false judgments fruits will fall.
At the end of the final world (there will be) a refuge to poverty and stinginess and grudging.

Wisdom will be turned into false judgments.
Great pride and great free-will will turn into the sons of peasants and churls.
Wrong judgments will pass into kings and lords.
Undutifulness and anger will pass into every one's mind, so that neither bondslaves nor handmaids will serve their masters; so that neither kings nor lords will hear the prayers of their tribes or their judgments...
Winter leafy, summer gloomy, autumn without crops, spring without flowers
Mortality with famine.
Failure on cornfields.
Flowers will perish.
In every house there will be wailing.

(Trans. By Whitley Stokes)

Ferchertne's prophecy is much longer than this, much of which makes no sense outside the context of ancient Irish society. Prophecies or other forms of mythology should not be taken too literally: the *Imbas* (power of prophecy) must be interpreted in the context of the prophet's own mental map of the world. This applies to both prophecies, and it opens up certain possibilities. What if we interpret these prophecies as referring to our own times, and what if we interpret them without making all of the same assumptions about society that the authors made?

If we look at the prophecies this way, we can see both danger and opportunity. Some of the things that seemed terrifying to whomever composed these prophecies could instead be interpreted as the first signs of a better new world that will come after the fall.

The Morrígan's prophecy could be summarized like this:

1- Environmental devastation. (Summer without flowers, Kine will be without milk... Woods without mast, Sea without produce...)

2- Collapse or overturning of traditional gender roles and sexual restrictions. (Women without modesty, Men without valour...)

3- Unjust laws and false legal judgments, both of which lead to loss of the Sovereignty in Irish belief. (Wrong judgments of old men, False precedents of brehons...)

4- A general collapse of social order. (Every man a betrayer, Every boy a reaver, etc.)

Ferchertne's prophecy could be summarized like this:

1- Environmental devastation, nature gone haywire. (The cattle of the world will be barren... Winter leafy, summer gloomy, autumn without crops, spring without flowers... Mortality with famine... Failure on corn-fields... Flowers will perish.)

2- Unjust laws, false legal judgments and unresponsive leaders too stingy to take care of the poor, leading to loss of the Sovereignty and the rejection of humanity by the Land. (Inhospitality will destroy flowers... Through false judgments fruits will fall... a refuge to poverty and stinginess and grudging... Wisdom will be turned into false judgments... Wrong judgments will pass into kings and lords... neither kings nor lords will hear the prayers of their tribes or their judgments...)

3- The downfall of traditional hierarchies, social leveling. (Every one will pass out of his proper state through pride and arrogance, so that neither rank nor old age, nor honour, nor dignity, nor art, nor instruction will be served... Every noble will be contemned: every baseborn will be set up... Great pride and great free-will will turn into the sons of peasants and churls... neither bondslaves nor handmaids will serve their masters...)

4- A general collapse of social order. (In every house there will be wailing, etc.)

When the leadership is corrupt and unresponsive, the Sovereignty is lost, the bounty and abundance of the natural world is withdrawn, and society drifts toward disaster. What if the collapse of hierarchy described in these prophecies is not just a consequence of the apocalypse but a way forward out of it? What if the collapse of traditional gender roles and class barriers is part of the new world the gods are making? What if the Sovereignty is passing out of the hands of our false leaders, not to a new leadership but to the people as a whole?

OUR TWO PROPHESIES

The prophesies of the Morrígan and Ferchertne promise terrible devastation, yet imply the possibility of a new beginning. If the downfall of our civilization is coming, it will not be the radicals who cause it. Indeed, we are almost the only ones who take it seriously enough to try to prevent it. Unlike the millennium promised by some mass-murdering prophet, our millennium will be one we did everything we could to hold back.

We should not seek to hasten the downfall of our civilization. Rather, we should devote ourselves to revolutionary change, without ever forgetting the sanctity of life as we do so. I believe that this is the only thing we can do to save our civilization from collapsing.

If it happens anyway, we should do what we can to make a better world out of whatever's left to us.

TO THE GODDESS OF THE CITY

In wooden beams, in bricks, in cobblestones
I see your face and feel your watching eyes.
And when the alleys moan
With wind I hear your cries.
You dance in every shaking sign
And drink when gutters run with spilled red wine.

You slip unnoticed in your all-night walk
Through empty playgrounds marked with fading chalk.
You sleep on benches in the winter cold
Forever growing old.
You see all secret things, and know all crimes
Committed on your streets. And you reveal
All things the wicked wish they could conceal.

When paper skitters down an empty street
At 3AM, I hear you walking past.
And I can hear the echoes of your feet
In sirens and in breaking glass.
Protect all those you pass along your way
And see them through until the light of day.

Oh goddess of my city, I am poor.
Keep hunger from my family's door.
Protect my neighbors from the storm
And keep us all well-fed and warm.
And I, in gratitude, will do the same
For others, in your name.

SEVEN

A CITY WHERE GODS CAN LIVE: PAGANISM AND URBAN LIBERATION

IMAGINE a city in some possible future. It's a beautiful place, not so much because of the architecture or layout, but because there are growing things everywhere. It doesn't look much like the cities of the past, but something more like a huge garden with buildings in it. Parts of it are completely forested and inhabited by wild animals. Others are given over to intensive crop cultivation. The rooftops and yards of every building are filled with vegetables and flowers. There are wells and streams of clean, clear water. In the large and open public squares, people of all types mingle freely to discuss local issues or daily events.

No two neighborhoods are the same: each has a distinctive personality and a different mix of cultures and religions. Not everyone is Pagan, but Pagan religious practices are fully accepted. Here and there throughout the city, you can see little shrines to different gods and spirits. There are sacred groves and holy trees, where people of any faith or no faith at all can go for spiritual renewal without fear of persecution.

The business of governing—if you want to call it that—is done on a neighborhood by neighborhood basis through directly democratic communes. Every person of every type has an equal voice, and an equal vote in the affairs of the commune. There are no bosses, although different people exercise leadership in different circumstances on an as-needed basis.

There is always work to do, from tending the vegetables or making clothing to keeping the streets clean or teaching the children, but there is no one forcing you to work for someone else's profit. Everyone contributes in whatever way seems best to the individual, and everyone shares in the city's wealth. There is no charge for food, or for a place to live, or for necessary health care. When there is a need for exchange, people treat it as an exchange of gifts.

People aren't alienated from each other, they live and work together in close proximity. If you have something you have to do, there is never any question that someone will watch the children. People sing while they work, or tell stories or jokes. As evening falls, people dance and socialize.

The lifestyle of the city is in some ways a simple one, not reliant on the constant use of high technology, but it isn't anti-technological. Technological knowledge is used extensively, but only in ways that will not disrupt the basic health and balance of the city's ecosystem.

Capitalism fell—perhaps hundreds of years ago—but civilization endures.

This is a utopian vision, I know. It's a fantasy of the imagination, but that doesn't make it a useless daydream. By imagining what my utopia would be, I free myself from what is. I give myself the power to start working immediately for a better world. If this is what my utopia would be like, then I know what steps will bring us closer.

THE ROJAVA REVOLUTION

When central government collapses, people must fend for themselves. This can be a disaster for everyone—or a precious opportunity.

In 2012, the dictatorial government of Bashar al-Assad lost control of the Kurdish regions in northern Syria because of the Syrian Civil War. Syrian troops stood down, and left a Kurdish militia known as the YPG or People's Protection Units in effective control. The YPG was the armed wing of the PYD or Democratic Union Party, a Syrian Kurdish political party allied with the PKK in neighboring Turkey. The PYD had been building up its network in the area for years, leaving it perfectly positioned to step in when Syrian troops pulled out.

Rather than establishing an ethnic nationalist state for the Kurds as they could so easily have done, the Democratic Union Party established a multi-ethnic autonomous region known as the Rojava Cantons, based on an explicitly ecological, feminist, and egalitarian philosophy called Democratic Confederalism.

While not an anarchist system in the strict sense, Democratic Confederalism was inspired by the writings of American anarchist philosopher Murray Bookchin. The Rojava Cantons are the largest and most successful political experiment in the anarchist tradition since the fall of Barcelona at the end of the Spanish Civil War.

From the moment the Rojava Cantons were established, they have been surrounded by absolutely ruthless enemies including Daesh, the Al-Nusra Front, and the Syrian and Turkish governments. Because of their desperate situation, they have been obliged to take allies wherever they can find them—earning the condemnation of some anarchists due to their military alliance with the United States. The courage and perseverance of the Kurdish militias has also thrilled and inspired people around the world, especially that of the Kurdish women's militia or YPJ.

The military situation simply is what it is: war makes for even stranger bedfellows than politics does. Rather than spending time on sterile debates about moral purity, I'd like to examine the system the Rojava Kurds have created. It may not be strictly anarchist, but it is unquestionably a move toward "power from below" and away from rule by bosses. It is also a step toward a new urban society, one that Pagan anarchists could happily help build.

DEMOCRATIC CONFEDERALISM

The political philosophy of the Rojava Cantons is Democratic Confederalism, which was first developed by imprisoned Kurdish revolutionary Abdullah Öcalan based on his correspondence with Murray Bookchin. Democratic Confederalism is applied through the Social Contract of the Rojava Cantons, which is essentially a Constitution.

This document opens with the statement that Rojava is a multi-ethnic society including "Kurds, Arabs, Syriacs, Arameans, Turkmen, Armenians and Chechens." Right at the outset, it rejects the idea of ethnic nationalism or separatism and proclaims that the revolutionary society will be based on "equality and environmental sustainability" with no interference from religious authorities in secular affairs. For a Pagan anarchist, this would be equivalent to a clear rejection of Folkish or so-called "National Anarchist" ideologies and an affirmation of egalitarian and ecological principles as the core of any future revolutionary change.

The Charter recognizes the full participation of "Kurdish, Arab, Syriac, Chechen, Armenian, Muslim, Christian and Yazidi communities peacefully co-existing in brotherhood." This is especially important for Pagan anarchists, because it represents a model for how a minority religion such as Paganism can be accommodated within a broader revolutionary framework.

The Yazidis are an ancient semi-Gnostic religious group, often misrepresented as Satanists because of the importance of a figure known as Malek T'aus, the Peacock Angel, in their mythology. The Peacock Angel is equivalent in some respects to Lucifer or Iblis, but the Yazidis understand this figure in a completely different way from Christians or Muslims. The Yazidis were targeted for genocide by Daesh because of their beliefs, and the YPG and YPJ militias were instrumental in rescuing the Yazidi community from annihilation.

For a majority-Muslim culture like the Kurds to come to the rescue of the Yazidis is a remarkable demonstration of their commitment to pluralism. A future social revolution in the Americas or Europe would likewise have to deal with the reality of seemingly incompatible belief systems existing side by side. Rather than promoting the hatred and rejection of Muslims, Christians, and atheists as some polytheist writers have done, we should emulate the Kurds and embrace a society of "Christian, Muslim, Jewish, Buddhist, Hindu, Sikh, Pagan and atheist people peacefully co-existing in solidarity."

The basic structure of the Charter is built around local self-government. According to "Democratic Confederalism in Kurdistan" by Tom Anderson:

> Looking more closely at these ideas, democratic confederalism is based on the idea that society can be run truly democratically through networks of grassroots assemblies or communes, which form confederations with each other across regions. Local assemblies elect representatives at the village or street level and these representatives represent their assembly at the level of the city or region. Again, the city or region elects representatives to represent them at higher levels... The idea is that the real power remains with the population, and not with state bureaucracies. According to Öcalan, a form of government would still be necessary, but only to implement the decisions made by the assemblies, whose representatives would be elected at a street or neighbourhood level.

A decentralized society of directly-democratic people's assemblies in confederation with each other is a basic goal of classical anarchism, so the anarchist roots of the Rojava Charter are clear. Democratic Confederalism isn't purely anarchist because it accepts the existence of a federated government to oversee the process. Classical anarchist thinkers such as Kropotkin would not have accepted this arrangement, as the federation of communes was intended to be a looser structure without governing authority over the individual communes. Democratic Confederalism also de-emphasizes class struggle, so it's unclear that the resulting society would really do away with the boss system. Despite this fact, collectivized worker cooperatives are common in Rojava and are seen as part of the revolutionary project.

In keeping with my preference for seeing anarchism as a critique rather than a system per se, I see Rojava as a huge step in the right direction for humanity. That doesn't and shouldn't mean that the Rojava Revolution is above all criticism, only that it is a positive step.

WOMEN IN ROJAVA

Islamophobes in the West often try to justify their bigotry with a hypocritical appeal to feminism—generally without any prior history of support for women's equality in our own society. According to their narrative, Islam is fundamentally and unchangeably misogynist, making it "incompatible with our values." Although Rojava is home to several different religious traditions, it is still majority Muslim. The Rojava Revolution demonstrates that a Muslim society can lead the way in the struggle for full equality under the right circumstances.

The Rojava Cantons are organized into communes of up to 300 people. Every commune has both a People's Council and a Women's Council. Each People's Council has two co-presidents, one male and one female. The People's Council decides on issues affecting the whole commune, and the Women's Council decides on issues affecting women specifically. The Women's Council can veto the decisions of the People's Council on women's issues. At every level of organization, women must make up at least 40 percent of every decision-making body.

It is difficult to imagine the sweeping social changes that would be necessary for a system this egalitarian to become the norm in any of the Liberal Democracies that are currently so concerned about Muslim immigration.

LIBERTARIAN MUNICIPALISM

I'm not suggesting that the Rojava Cantons are anything like the fantasy city I described at the beginning of this chapter. However, they are much closer to that vision than our current situation. Over hundreds of years, a society like the Rojava Cantons could develop in the direction of that ideal city, assuming it could survive while also remaining true to its founding values. If we want to make our society a better place for every living being, we need not only the pragmatism to solve daily problems but also the idealism to dream of long-term goals. We have to be clear on what the ideal society would be like if we want to achieve even a reasonably good society today.

Murray Bookchin provides some useful ideas to help get us started down this path, but we cannot stop with Murray Bookchin. For one thing, Bookchin had an intense and somewhat inexplicable disdain for Paganism. He dismissed any combination of Pagan and anarchist ideas as mere "lifestyle anarchism," divorced from the tradition of revolutionary struggle.

Bookchin's philosophy of "social ecology" and "libertarian municipalism" was based on urban living rather than the hunter-gatherer lifestyle espoused by anarcho-primitivists. Bookchin was inspired by the ancient Greek polis and the notion of the informed and politically engaged citizen of the polis. A society based on Bookchin's ideas would be made up of autonomous directly-democratic cities. Bookchin conceived of these cities as ecologically-oriented, but rejected any revival of animism or Pagan religion.

In *Beyond Bookchin: Preface for a Future Social Ecology*, David Watson systematically dissected every aspect of Bookchin's philosophy, concluding that Bookchin's ideas have little to offer the future and should be set aside. Watson particularly objected to Bookchin's reductionist materialism, arguing for the value of primal and indigenous worldviews—including their animistic and mythopoetic aspects. Watson was an early advocate of anarcho-primitivism, although he later criticized what he saw as the excesses of this movement.

Obviously Watson did not foresee that Bookchin's ideas would provide the inspiration for a revolutionary new society. The existence of the Rojava Cantons basically vindicates Bookchin—his philosophy has legs. However, many of Watson's specific criticisms will probably resonate with Pagan anarchists. Social ecology without a spiritual dimension seems like an abstract theory; it's not based deeply in relationship between people and their landscape.

Bookchin's dismissal of indigenous societies ignores the fact that people living in this way have been so much more successful at not destroying their environments than we have. Bookchin is no doubt correct that some primitivists romanticize primal societies in ways that are basically condescending "Noble Savage" racism. That doesn't mean he's correct that we should disregard and dismiss their ways of life, or the value of their spiritual perspective for creating a truly ecological society of the future.

As Watson says:

An evolved reason will have a place for the wolf, for the consciousness of the redwood, for ghost dancers, mystics and animistic tribal villagers – will coax into being, with a little luck, a rounded, vital synthesis of archaic and modern.

My daydream of the ideal city is meant as a baby step toward such a synthesis.

OH YOU MOTHERS

This is the prayer I use when leaving offerings for my own ancestors.

Oh you mothers, all my mothers
Those who sleep in heavy soil,
Those who went to death so weary
All you thought was no more toil,
Those who danced with joy and laughter,
Those who fought to break the chains
Though you'll know no more hereafters,
Here a part of you remains.

Oh you fathers, all my fathers
Those who dream in wet, black earth,
Those who let their dreams go hungry
So that mine could come to birth,
Those who died in rage and sorrow
Those who laughed and wandered free,
Though you'll know no more tomorrows
Your tomorrows live in me.

All of you who came before me,
Though I know your names or not.
All who added to my story
Giving blood or deed or thought.
Take this food and drink I give you,
Share it with me, take your fill.
Though your verses may have ended
Yet the song continues still.

EIGHT

MY FAMILIAR IS SABOCAT!

THE trade guilds of medieval Europe were more than just professional bodies. They had a religious function, too. Guilds were usually dedicated to a particular saint, and one of the main activities of a guild was to organize religious pageants and mystery plays.

This is one of several points of connection between the medieval guilds and the ancient collegia of Pagan Europe. Throughout the territories of the Roman Empire, people organized collegia or social clubs for various purposes. Many of these clubs were strictly burial societies, pooling their resources to make sure all the members could afford a decent funeral. Many of them were guild-like organizations of trade professionals—in the city of Rome, there were collegia of sutlers, chair-makers, garbage collectors, actors, gladiators, and so on.

Some collegia were religious, including the four officially-recognized orders of the Roman priesthood, and others without official status, such as the collegium of Bacchus banned by law in 186 and 64 BC. The collegium of Bacchus probably continued to exist as an underground organization while under the ban. Unlicensed and illegal collegia were known as *collegia illicita*, a phrase that can be translated as "unlawful assemblies" (words that should sound familiar to any modern activist!). Some of these *collegia illicita* were mafia-like organizations, others were underground religious groups (such as the Christians), and some were secret political organizations.

According to *Christianity and the Roman Government: A Study in Imperial Administration* by Ernest George Hardy, *collegia illicita* were not usually harshly suppressed unless they engaged in subversive political activities. The fact that they often did so is shown by the fact that *collegia illicita* were suppressed after public disturbances on several occasions, and that the word illicitum became a synonym for "political."

In the collegia of ancient times, we have the model for an organization that could function as a trade union, a mutual aid society, a worship circle dedicated to a particular god or goddess, or an underground revolutionary cell. No single ancient collegia that I am aware of combined all these functions at once, but just imagine they had! The result would have been something like a Pagan anarcho-syndicalism.

FIGHTING WORDS

Anarcho-syndicalism is revolutionary unionism, as represented by the great anarchist and syndicalist trade unions of history such as the IWW and the CNT. The anarcho-syndicalist flag is the familiar black and red flag, now used by many anti-fascist streetfighters. I once carried this flag in an IWW march during Occupy Minnesota, where the IWW activists chanted slogans that sounded obsolete to me at the time. "We don't need no bosses, let the workers run the shop!" had a 1930s vibe, suggesting old black and white photos of grim-faced strikers staring down the state militia.

Organizations like the IWW have history behind them, but that doesn't mean their ideas are behind the times. The more I thought about it, the more their slogan rang true. I liked some of my bosses and disliked others, but I couldn't think of a single boss whose guidance or "supervision" had actually helped me do my job in any way, except for when I was 19 and working at a day care. In every other workplace, a good boss was one who stayed out of the way and a bad boss was one who tried to manage me and made it difficult for me to do my job effectively.

In Liberal Democracies, we claim to believe that people should choose their own leaders when it comes to government, but we accept arbitrary dictatorship in the workplace. This makes no sense. If democracy is the best way for a group of people to make decisions, it ought to be best for the workplace as well. This is especially true when we spend more of our waking hours at work than anywhere else. By the same logic, if I support the reorganization of society into decentralized communes with directly-democratic processes, then I should support the same mode of organization in the workplace too. Turns out, I'm an anarcho-syndicalist.

According to the Workers' Solidarity Alliance (a modern anarcho-syndicalist organization):

> To liberate itself from subordination to dominating classes, the working class must dismantle the hierarchical structures of the corporations and the state. The working class, through its own united action, must seize and manage directly the entire system of production, distribution and services.
> Self-management must not be limited to the workplaces but must be extended throughout the society and to governance of public affairs. Self-management means that people control the decisions that affect them. The basic building blocks of a self-managed society would be assemblies of workers in workplaces and of residents in neighborhoods. These assemblies would be federated together throughout society.

This is classical anarcho-communism, with a particular focus on the revolutionary role of the trade union. Syndicalist trade unions are very different from the AFL-CIO or the Teamsters. They don't have a strong internal bureaucracy or hierarchy with careerist officials, and power is decentralized to the local union chapters. They don't create separate unions for separate trades; instead, they follow the "one big union" philosophy of the IWW and CNT, so that employers can't turn the different unions against each other.

The Industrial Workers of the World, or IWW, was once a powerful organization with tens of thousands of members in the United States, Canada, and Australia. The movement in the U.S. was practically destroyed by government repression before World War II—including long prison sentences and murder by lynch mob. Somehow it held on and still exists to this day, with the IWW playing a prominent role in Occupy Minnesota and staging militant actions in support of Black Lives Matter.

Spain's Confederación Nacional del Trabajo, or CNT, took over Catalonia in 1936, staging the most comprehensive anarchist revolution to date. Eventually crushed by the Stalinists and then by the Fascists, the CNT held on as a resistance organization through the Franco years and then revived after the end of the dictatorship. Like the IWW, it carries on, although without the mass membership it once enjoyed.

The high-point of anarcho-syndicalism was over by the beginning of the Second World War, and modern anarcho-syndicalist organizations are all much smaller than their predecessors. Perhaps the movement will never regain its former strength, but the fact remains that this branch of anarchism has achieved more tangible results than any other. Anarchist Spain was a reality, however briefly. Barcelona was once an anarchist city.

WILDCAT!

Rebellion is as the sin of witchcraft. – I Samuel xv, 23.

One of the most recognizable symbols of the IWW is the screeching black wild cat, a symbol of the wildcat strike and acts of sabotage against employers. The IWW wild cat is known as Sabocat or Sabo-Tabby. According to folklorist Archie Green (as quoted on the IWW website):

> "(T)he black cat is an old symbol for malignant and sinister purposes, foul deeds, bad luck, and witchcraft with countless superstitious connections. Wobblies extended the black-cat figure visually to striking on the job, direct action, and sabotage."

According to oral tradition, Sabocat was a feral black cat adopted by struggling IWW lumberjacks under siege from company thugs. The wild cat came into the striker's camp looking more than half dead, but the strikers nursed him back to health. As the cat got fatter, the strikers started to win more fights—a clear case of sympathetic magic!

Ralph Chaplin, who designed the symbol, intended it to represent sabotage only in the economic sense—worker slow-downs intended to sabotage corporate profits. IWW propaganda posters showed the black cat along with the slogan *"Beware Sabotage—Good Pay or Bum Work."*

However, other members of the IWW sometimes interpreted the symbol to refer to literal acts of sabotage. The IWW today insists that Sabocat represents only "direct action at the point of production," or "Collective Withdrawal of Efficiency," not the deliberate destruction of company equipment. When the government cracked down on the IWW during World War I, the Wobblies were accused of tree-spiking, arson, and dynamite attacks. They steadfastly insisted that Sabocat only represented the worker slow-down, but were convicted anyway.

The Sabocat symbol proved popular with anarchists in general, and appears on some CNT propaganda as well. Over time it came to be used as a catch-all symbol for direct action. In the 1980s, environmentalist militants in Earth First! started to use the symbol for tree-spiking and other forms of "ecotage." Some chapters of the IWW had close ties and shared membership with Earth First! at the time, yet IWW members of Earth First! such as Judi Bari were outspoken opponents of tree-spiking and other ecotage tactics. To this day, the IWW disavows any use of Sabocat as a symbol of ecotage or monkeywrenching.

Hidden Folk

The Earth Liberation Front was founded in 1992 by UK members of Earth First! The ELF is a leaderless resistance movement, so individual cells have no contact with or knowledge of each other. ELF cells have carried out a number of arson and ecotage attacks all over the world. In 2001, the Federal Bureau of Investigation declared ELF the number one domestic terrorist group despite the fact that no ELF action had ever resulted in loss of life—a clear indication of how much the State values property and profit above human beings. You don't have to condone ELF's tactics to agree that "terrorism" should be defined as actions intended to terrorize, not merely to sabotage.

Members of ELF are known as "Elves." This is especially appropriate from a Pagan perspective, as real elves and similar fairy creatures are also known for acts of sabotage. For instance, Álfhóll, a traditional elf hill in Iceland, was set to be demolished because of road work in the 1930s, but the route was altered when tools and equipment were mysteriously damaged. The same thing happened again in the 1980s, and Álfhóll is now a protected site. Similarly, the failure of the DeLorean factory in Ireland was popularly attributed to the thoughtless cutting-down of a local fairy tree during construction of the site. More recently in Iceland, seers claiming to speak for the elves have been arrested in environmental protests.

Of course, this is all very different from the more extreme tactics used by ELF. However, an ELF cell could be seen as a *collegium illicitum* in the ancient Roman sense, an "unlawful assembly" of people acting for a combination of political and spiritual purposes.

THE BLACK CAT COMES BACK

Even if you reject the tactics used by ELF or Earth First! because of the danger that people could be hurt, the legacy of Sabocat may still have a role to play. Leland's *Aradia* presents this account of the origins of witch-craft:

> This is the Gospel (Vangelo) of the Witches:
>
> Diana greatly loved her brother Lucifer, the god of the Sun and of the Moon, the god of Light (Splendor), who was so proud of his beauty, and who for his pride was driven from Paradise.
>
> Diana had by her brother a daughter, to whom they gave the name of Aradia...
>
> In those days there were on earth many rich and many poor.
>
> The rich made slaves of all the poor.
>
> In those days were many slaves who were cruelly treated; in every palace tortures, in every castle prisoners.
>
> Many slaves escaped. They fled to the country; thus they became thieves and evil folk. Instead of sleeping by night, they plotted escape and robbed their masters, and then slew them. So they dwelt in the mountains and forests as robbers and assassins, all to avoid slavery...
>
> Diana said one day to her daughter Aradia:
>
> 'Tis true indeed that thou a spirit art,
> But thou wert born but to become again
> A mortal; thou must go to earth below
> To be a teacher unto women and men
> Who fain would study witchcraft in thy school...
>
> And thou shalt be the first of witches known;
> And thou shalt be the first of all i' the world;
> And thou shalt teach the art of poisoning,
> Of poisoning those who are great lords of all;
> Yea, thou shalt make them die in their palaces;
> And thou shalt bind the oppressor's soul (with power);
> And when ye find a peasant who is rich,
> Then ye shall teach the witch, your pupil, how

To ruin all his crops with tempests dire,
With lightning and with thunder (terrible),
And the hall and wind....

This is not a form of witchcraft based on the "Rule of Three," to put it mildly! This is revolutionary witchcraft, magic as a weapon of class warfare. If we believe that our magic works, then we ought to use it. We ought to wage magical warfare on the system of capitalism, not in preference to more direct forms of direct action but in tandem with them.

RE-ENCHANTING THE REVOLUTION

Dr. Bones, a noted disciple of individualist anarchist Max Stirner, has written many articles about the connection between Stirner's Egoism and the practical use of magic. Practical magic or witchcraft is personal power, freed from the "spooks" of Thou Shalt Not and "An It Harm None, Do As Ye Will."

> "Magic presupposes we can change the foundations of the world around us. Why do our political beliefs so often not follow this maxim? Why are we waiting for some Vanguard, some Party, some Candidate, to rip up the noxious weeds of Capitalism and The State? Did we come by any of our magical knowledge by waiting or did we simply go out and start doing what we could? Wasn't every bump in the road a lesson, every victory a confirmation that even against the odds we can win?
> My tradition courses through the land and was born in struggle: against the State, against the Boss, against the Police. Under candle light and shroud of burning herbs I can feel the air thick with those that whispered or sang prayers in other times; they know, they understand: the battles may be different, the symbols may have changed, but the struggle has not. Candle flames burst with the same heat and energy raging away in my heart, teeth gritting in Nietzschean Will to change the world and break anything that stands in my way. Road Opener work or Revolution, what's the difference?"
> (From: "Folk Magick as Insurrection" by Dr. Bones)

Just as the fighters of the CNT defense committees struck back at the pistoleros of Barcelona's employing class, the witch or root doctor can strike back through magical means at an exploitative boss or violent police officer. Pacifism and "Harm None" serves the interests of the rich and powerful, and can never liberate anyone. The hex is an ancient tool to give power to the powerless. But does the magic really work? Try it for yourself and find out!

REVOLUTIONARY MAGIC

Dr. Bones has written extensively on the folk magic tradition known as Hoodoo, and how it can be used for resistance magic. Peter Grey's *Apocalyptic Witchcraft* and other works from Scarlet Imprint Press present a version of witchcraft far removed from the "Rule of Three." Another useful source of information—especially for anti-capitalist heathens—is *The Sorcerer's Screed*, a fascinating twentieth-century grimoire from Iceland.

The author was a man named Jochum Magnus Eggertsson, although he went by the name Skuggi, which means "Shadow." As is often the case with traditional grimoires, not all of the workings described by Skuggi can be considered ethical. The interesting point about this particular work is why the author created it, after he had spent about thirty years tracking down old Icelandic manuscripts for information about the occult. In his preface and conclusion, Skuggi expresses his bitterness toward the civic and clerical authorities in Iceland, stating that the clergy were "in fact funded by capitalism, here as elsewhere, to deliver predetermined sermons for a predetermined price...".

Skuggi apparently put the book together because he wanted to give people a sense that they had power of their own, independent of either the secular or sacred authorities. The spells in *The Sorcerer's Screed* call on the Christian God and the old heathen gods with equal ease. The author himself seems to have embraced a doctrine of polytheistic monism, stating that the gods are "infinitely many, yet one..." and that the study of magic was one way to become like the gods.

> **Whether you have a formal teacher in the traditional sense or not, magic is something you learn by doing.**

A classic source of revolutionary magic is the *Aradia*, Leland's work on Italian witchcraft. Regardless of the real origins of this fascinating work, it presents a form of witchcraft practice with explicitly radical politics.

Although you can get started in revolutionary magic with any of these works, there is no substitute for experience. Whether you have a formal teacher in the traditional sense or not, magic is something you learn by doing.

UNLAWFUL ASSEMBLIES

Out of all the modern writers on witchcraft, Montague Summers is probably the strangest. A believer in the literal reality of everything found in the witchcraft trial records, Summers repeatedly described witchcraft as a revolutionary conspiracy of medieval anarchists.

I'm not suggesting he was right, but just imagine he was. Imagine that some *collegium illicitum* devoted to Diana and Aradia survived underground somehow as a peasant's resistance movement, giving rise to the legend of the witch—and eventually gifting the symbol of the witch's black cat to the anarcho-syndicalists of the IWW and the CNT. I don't believe this is factually true, but it makes a wonderful myth!

It's also a myth we can make true today. A coven can function as a revolutionary cell, simultaneously practicing Pagan religion, direct action, and radical witchcraft. A druidic grove can engage in worship, magical practice, and environmental protest. Solitary practitioners can carry out magical attacks and participate in protest actions. We can take inspiration from the *collegia illicita* of ancient Paganism, offering each other mutual aid and worshiping together as we resist the systems destroying our planet.

With respect for the history of the design and of the IWW, Sabocat is an ideal symbol for Pagan anarchists involved in direct action. The black cat's connections to witchcraft are old and powerful, and the folklore about the black cat rescued by striking lumberjacks suggests ancient legends of divine intervention. In myths of this type, the deity appears in the guise of a person or animal in need, and reveals its power only if first offered aid by human beings—just like the story, in which the strikers started to win their battles only after feeding the hungry black cat.

For a revolutionary witch, Sabocat makes the perfect familiar.

CURSE
TABLET

I write these words on sheets of lead
And leave them in a dead man's hands
To bring them to the silent lands

Of root and water, and of rot.
I whisper them into the ear
Of one who can no longer hear.

I show them to the gaping eyes
Of one who lies beneath the leaves.
Oh gods of dread who punish thieves,

Leave off all lesser punishments and hear!
The thieves who rule the world have gorged
On others' bread and meat. They've forged

New manacles to bind the wrists
Of any who resist. They kill
Whoever will not do their will.

Oh gods who dwell beneath the earth,
Arise tonight and hunt for prey
More worthy of your power. Slay

The kings of thieves, the lords of men,
And not the poor who steal their bread.
I write this curse on sheets of lead

And leave them in a dead man's hands.
I whisper them into the ear
Of those who sleep, but always hear.

I show them to the empty eyes
Of those who lie beneath the leaves,
Oh gods of dread who punish thieves!

NINE

MANY GODS, NO MASTERS

THE phrase "No Gods, No Masters" has appeared on many banners and been carried proudly in front of many protest marches since it was first used by the Industrial Workers of the World during the famous "Bread and Roses" strike of 1912. These words express the refusal to bow down to any person or institution, a defiance echoed in the anarchist slogan "Whoever they vote for, we are ungovernable."

Marching behind these defiant slogans with the rest of the crowd, there is the occasional Pagan anarchist, wearing a black shirt with a different slogan: "Many Gods, No Masters." Is this a fundamental contradiction? Is a god necessarily a master—or can a god be a liberator?

The traditional anarchist slogan "No Gods, No Masters" depends on a particular interpretation of what a god is. The slogan assumes that there are actually no gods, and that what we call a god is really an illusion, a trick, a false mental construct designed to manipulate people into placid obedience. If you believe what most religions tell you about the gods they worship, the gods want you to obediently serve your earthly masters. You must "render unto Caesar," no matter what Caesar does with what you render him. Your masters may someday face divine judgment for their crimes: but always later, never today.

It's a cynical trap, an enchantment that silences those who would speak up against oppression and paralyzes those who would raise their hands to fight it. As soon as you realize there is no god, there is also no master, because you've banished the ghost of the master from your own consciousness. "No Gods, No Masters" is a liberating slogan, if we're only talking about that sort of god.

99% BRIGHID

The year 2011 saw massive uprisings and popular protests all over the world in the name of radical democracy and against the corporate state. From October 2011 onward, I was personally involved in these struggles as an activist for Occupy Minnesota. Given the reputation of Minneapolis as "Paganistan," it's not surprising that a few of my fellow Occupiers were Pagans, but others were Christian and quite a few were atheists.

I remember being particularly moved at a foreclosure defense action when one of the scheduled speakers expressed his commitment to social justice with the phrase "The Earth is the Lord's" and got a roar of appreciation from the blue-collar crowd. The Earth is the Lord's—not just a commodity to be owned and controlled by a few powerful men, but a "common treasury" as the 17th century Christian radicals known as the Diggers put it. That's how a Christian expressed his understanding of Occupy and what it stood for. So how would a Pagan do the same?

In polytheistic religions, there's hypothetically a deity for everything, but one would assume that the Iron Age Celts did not get around to naming a deity of social justice and radical activism. One would not be entirely correct, however, as several of the myths associated with Brighid have a radical theme.

Brighid is one of the most enduringly popular deities of ancient Irish myth. In Her most well-known form, She appears as three sisters, all named Brighid, the goddesses of poetry, healing, and smithcraft. All three are associated with fire and water. Daughters of a boisterous god called the Dagda, these three Brighids are remembered for their wisdom and healing powers. The poets of ancient Ireland considered Brighid their protector. According to an ancient text called *Cormac's Glossary*, Brighid was so popular and powerful that many different Irish goddesses were given this name. Some of these lesser-known Brighids are associated with issues of social justice.

Consider Brig Ambue, "Brighid of the Cowless." Cows equaled wealth in ancient Celtic society, where your legal worth was officially measured by how many cattle a person must pay your tribe if he killed you. To be *ambue* or "cowless" was to be worth absolutely nothing: the *ambue* were the dispossessed, and Brig Ambue was their protector. When desperate warriors of the ambue class staged cattle raids to support their families, Brig Ambue was invoked in cleansing rituals to absolve them of guilt and reintegrate them into community life.

Brig Ambue was said to be the daughter of the great judge Sencha. The only false judgment Sencha was said to ever have made was denying women the right to inherit land in their own name. His daughter Brig Ambue denounced his judgment, and three blisters appeared on his face as soon as she spoke. They disappeared again only when he ruled in favor of the rights of women.

Brig Ambue's mother was Brig Brethach or "Brighid of Judgment," and this Brighid is also associated with legal judgments on behalf of women. Brig Ambue's grandmother was Brig Briugu, whose name means "Brighid of Hospitality."

If a person of common origins acquired enough wealth in ancient Ireland, he could achieve noble status by becoming a *briugu* or hosteler. Hostelers maintained roadside inns where any traveler could stable his horses, sleep in a warm bed, eat a hot meal, and drink his fill of the local beer, all absolutely free. Hostelers were expected to have enough wealth of their own to set up shop, but the hostel was supported by the tribal king out of the cattle he was paid in tribute. In other words, they were socialized travel hotels. Their purpose was to facilitate trade by making travel easier, safer, and less expensive—but also to fulfill the principle of unconditional hospitality, a central and sacred obligation in ancient Celtic society. Brig Briugu's role as a mythical hosteler was reflected in the later legends of St. Brigit magically brewing limitless quantities of beer or giving away food to the poor.

Brig Ambue, Brig Briugu, and Brig Brethach are three of the more obscure avatars or manifestations of Brighid in ancient Ireland, but the themes they are concerned with are consistently radical in modern terms: justice for the dispossessed, food and shelter without charge for those in need, and the rights of women. One might assume that these themes would have been diminished when the goddess Brighid became St. Brigit with the introduction of Christianity, but in fact they were amplified.

According to the legend of St. Brigit, she was the daughter of a slave and the tribal chief who owned her, an implicit critique of the slave economy of the ancient world and of the sexual exploitation of slaves. She was not, however, a very meek or obedient slave. On the contrary, she made a habit of giving away her father's food, drink, and prized possessions to the poor at every opportunity. When he became so frustrated at her constant redistribution of his wealth that he tried to give her away to the king, she gave his sword to a passing beggar while waiting outside in his chariot. The king, perhaps wisely, refused to take her.

St. Brigit continued her policy of constant hospitality and wealth redistribution as the abbess of Kildare, though she often used her saintly powers to restore whatever had been given away. A number of legends portray her tense relationship with Ailill, the king of Leinster, reflecting the earlier status of the goddess as the personified Sovereignty of that province. St. Brigit was willing to lend her powers to the king, but only on condition that he free his slave.

She offered to guarantee him good children, a dynasty of his own, and entrance into Heaven for himself, but he refused all of it. The only thing Ailill cared about was victory in battle against the tribes of Ulster, but he was willing to free the slave if St. Brigit would promise him that. This is important because it once again confirms that St. Brigit had inherited the role of the goddess of the Land, whose duties in the ancient Pagan religion included supporting the tribe in battle. Unlike the Morrígan, another Land goddess who is described as being downright bloodthirsty, St. Brigit is only portrayed as aiding the Leinster army when Leinster was being invaded by a hostile force. Brighid serves as a battle goddess only to defend the land and its people, not to engage in acts of aggression.

In the Celtic lore of the Land or Sovereignty goddess, the goddess grants the kingship to the tribal king by offering him a drink of mead from Her own hands. Only when he drinks from the hands of the goddess who personifies the tribal territory does he become the king. In one of the legends of St. Brigit, she gives away all of the mead intended for the king's visit to entertain the common people of the tribe. Though often interpreted as another story about the saint's tender concern for the poor, in context of her role as a stand-in for the Leinster goddess, it has a clear political implication: the saint or goddess takes the drink of Sovereignty away from the king and gives it to the common people.

She later magically restores the mead to the king, but the warning message remains. The Sovereignty of the land belongs to the goddess, not the king. "The Earth is the Lady's." If he proves to be an unjust ruler, She has it within Her power to take his authority away and give it directly to the common people.

In the case of Brighid, we have a goddess who protects the poor, frees slaves, and defies kings. A liberator, not a master. And she's not the only one.

I AM SPARTACUS!

In *The Spartacus War*, historian Barry Strauss describes the ancient religion of Dionysus:

> To the downtrodden, Dionysus offered hope; to the Roman ruling class he spelled trouble. They associated him with southern Italy and Sicily, where the god was especially popular, and where rebels had fought under the banner of Dionysus over the years...
>
> In 186 B.C., the Roman Senate claimed that Italy's widespread Dionysiac groups masked a conspiracy. In an atmosphere of fear and panic, the Senate launched a witch hunt up and down the peninsula and drove Romans from the cult...
>
> Dionysus was left to the powerless of Italy and they embraced him... Between 135 and 101 B.C., two slave revolts in Sicily and one slave revolt in western Anatolia all invoked Dionysus. The god appeared again in the revolt of Rome's Italian allies known as the Social War... rebel coins showed Bacchus as symbol of liberation.

When Spartacus began his legendary uprising, he was accompanied and supported by a priestess of Dionysus, a prophetess known only as "the Thracian Lady." According to the prophecies of this revolutionary maenad, Spartacus enjoyed the divine favor of Dionysus for the revolt—the god had imbued him with "a great and fearful power" to smite the Roman authorities. That's exactly what he did, winning one victory after another against the Roman legions.

Many of the rebel gladiator's followers were Celtic slaves, who would not have been particularly familiar with Dionysus. They had priestesses of their own, such as the two who were interrupted by Roman soldiers while making an offering to the Celtic gods on behalf of the uprising. As Strauss says, "religion encouraged a spirit of resistance, as the Celtic women show." The two druidesses slipped back to camp and warned the rebels of the Roman advance.

The religion of Dionysus was a revolutionary faith, a creed directly associated with the struggle against slavery and oppression.

Spartacus was eventually defeated and killed, and his followers were crucified *en masse*. Yet it is clear from Strauss's history that the religion of Dionysus was a revolutionary faith, a creed directly associated with the struggle against slavery and oppression.

In later years, the Romans did tolerate a revived form of the Dionysian religion, stripped of its radical associations. Apolitical polytheism, then as now, was conservative by default. That doesn't change the radical history of this god's worship—it only veils it.

Still, how could Dionysus be a patron of both royal dynasties and rebel slaves?

GODS AND ARCHONS

Anarchists sometimes have a hard time reconciling their commitment to atheism with their commitment to anti-colonialism. For example, consider this passage from *Anarchism vs. Primitivism* by Brian Oliver Sheppard:

> *Most, if not all, native societies practiced some type of religion. The rich variety of Native American creation myths is known to many. Anarchism, by contrast, has traditionally posited atheism — in fact, antitheism — as the only belief system congruent with the scientific understanding of reality... (P)agan beliefs (or delusions) were widely held by other hunter-gatherer cultures... Of course, this does not mean that anarchists wish to forcibly impose atheism on others. In an anarchist society, people would be free to believe whatever they wanted. But an anarchist society worthy of the name would not allow those holding religious beliefs to impose them upon others, nor would religious beliefs be allowed to influence decisions of production and distribution. Although individual belief in mystical forces would be tolerated, most anarchists would probably continue to criticize the irrationality of those who believed in the supernatural.*

Despite the claim that anarchists would not "impose atheism" on anyone, the passage reeks of disdain for the "superstitious" beliefs of "primitive" peoples. It would also rob any future anarchist society of one of the greatest strengths Paganism could otherwise give it: the animist reverence for the natural world. If mythic beliefs must not be allowed to influence "decisions of production and distribution," then the whole earth could very well be covered with anarchist factories instead of capitalist ones.

Anarcho-primitivists who insist on atheism face a similar problem, as the societies they emulate were and are far from atheist. Any anarchist who takes the primitivist critique seriously must also seriously consider the role of myth and spirituality in creating a healthier society for the future. This can only work if there is more to the concept of a "god" than what is implied in the phrase "No Gods, No Masters."

In the essay "Gods and Politics, Warp and Weft" on Gods and Radicals, Yvonne Aburrow writes:

A deity is a powerful entity or identity who has emerged from the complexity of the universe, and is shaped by social interactions (with humans, animals, their environment, other deities, and other spirit entities) just as humans are. Deities have agency, or at least they seem to. Often that agency involves influencing people to do their work for them.

If there are many deities, then it stands to reason that different deities would have different goals in mind and would influence humans to do different things. If a deity is like a person in some sense, then different deities would have different relationships with human beings. In fact, it would be reasonable to assume that no two devotional relationships would be exactly the same.

In modern polytheism, we do actually see a wide range of different relationships between the gods and their devotees. Some people are interested in or inspired by the mythology of a particular deity but never experience any kind of personal contact. It would only be natural for them to think of the deity primarily as a metaphor or archetype, as atheist Pagans do.

Some people have dreams of a deity or even waking visions. Some enter ecstatic trance states in communion with their gods. Some feel that their deities communicate with them through signs and omens. Some think of the deity as a passionate lover, some as a parental figure, some as a friend. Some people experience their gods as wrathful masters, giving orders and making threats. The same deity can appear as a friend and equal to one person and as an angry master to another.

This seems to be true of all sorts of gods, not just the deities we consider Pagan. The organized religions have a lot to say about transformative mystical experiences that happened to other people in the distant past, but they usually discourage us from seeking mystical experiences of our own. When they can't discourage mysticism effectively, they try to channel it into approved patterns. Christian literature on mysticism constantly warns the reader that any visions or ecstasies outside the boundaries of orthodoxy can only come from Satan. Despite these warnings, some Christian mystics have dared to step outside the approved guidelines.

In 1649, Christian radical Gerrard Winstanley called for a peaceful revolution to "level" all social classes and make the earth into a common treasury for all. Where did he get this notion? In his own words:

This work to make the Earth a Common Treasury, was shewed us by Voice in Trance, and out of Trance, which words were these, "Work together, Eate Bread together, Declare this all abroad."

Instead of accepting established doctrine, Winstanley went directly to the source. In trances and in visions, he sought direct contact with the god of the Christian faith, and what his god told him was not to obey his masters but to resist their power.

So we have the god who spoke to Winstanley, telling him and the other Diggers to make the earth into a common treasury for all. And we have the god of Oliver Cromwell, who sent his soldiers to destroy what the Diggers had built. At least in theory, these were both the same god. But why would the same god inspire two completely different ways of living?

Even if a god is in some sense a person, the gods are much vaster than human people. Every god appears differently in different contexts; every god has aspects. By choosing how to engage with the god, we choose how to bring that god into our world. Fire remains fire whether it warms or burns.

In his essay "Worlding the Gods," Rhyd Wildermuth writes:

> The gods exist as independent beings from us regardless of our belief in them. But it's we who actually world them into the earth, and how we world them is dependent upon what we do, who we are, and the sort of world we create around us... The true offering we give to the gods, which is precisely the same offering we give to any other living being, is this act of worlding. When I make offerings to Arianrhod, she's not drinking that mead. Instead, by offering her mead or flowers, I am worlding her into the earth through the act of offering those things...

The gods are spiritual powers—vast, numinous energies—and we cannot possibly know what they are in themselves. They show themselves to us through the filter of our minds, through the ways we dream of them and the ways we imagine them. They maintain relationships with human beings and seemingly influence humans in various ways, but we humans influence the gods as well.

When we pray to Dionysus to help us fight oppression with the courage of Spartacus, we world Dionysus as a liberator. When we pray to Brighid to give us Brig Ambue's guidance in the quest for justice, we world Brighid as a liberator. However, there are those who world the gods as tyrants.

In ancient Gnosticism, powerful Archons or "rulers" stand in the way of our spiritual development, blocking our access to gnosis or enlightenment. There were many systems of Gnosticism with different teachings, but several of them equate the Archons with the "seven planets" of ancient astronomy: the sun, the moon, Mercury, Venus, Mars, Jupiter, and Saturn. According to the Ophite sect, the Archon of Saturn was identical with the god of the Old Testament, a false creator or Demiurge, a tyrant obsessed with demanding obedience. In some of the Gnostic systems there are hundreds of Archons, all of them tyrants who seek to prevent humanity from fulfilling its spiritual potential.

> **If we dream them as liberators, then the gods can liberate us. They can inspire us to rebel like Spartacus and defend the rights of the oppressed like Brighid.**

If the god of the Bible is always and only a loving benefactor, he could scarcely have inspired this legend of a wrathful tyrant and false creator. If he is always and only a tyrannical demiurge, he would never have told Gerrard Winstanley to make the earth into a common treasury.

If we dream them as liberators, then the gods can liberate us. They can inspire us to rebel like Spartacus and defend the rights of the oppressed like Brighid. They can speak out in the voice of trance to tell us to make the earth into a common treasury.

If we dream them as tyrannical masters, then the gods can become Archons, cruel guardians who prevent us from tasting gnosis.

In all of this, I believe that the gods themselves simply are what they are. We do not control them and we can never tame them. However, a god is simply too vast and powerful to be seen all at once, so by thinking of the gods from one angle or another we effectively choose which part of them to invite in.

The decision is ours. The gods are Archons if we world them as Archons, liberators if we world them as liberators.

So let us choose!

APPENDIX: PRACTICE, NOT ORTHOPRAXY

A PAGAN RITUAL

This ritual is designed to include the most essential elements of Pagan practice, including the creation of sacred space, honoring the spirits of nature, ancestor veneration, and leaving offerings to deities. It avoids ritual formats associated with specific traditions such as Wicca or Asatru, so that pagans of many different traditions will be equally comfortable worshiping together in this format.

It also avoids the hierarchies found in some traditions. This ritual is designed to treat all participants as equals, and to give each of them an equal opportunity to pray and speak. The role of priest can be played by any participant with the necessary skills and should not be treated as a fixed title or rank. The best practice would probably be to rotate the role or to assign a different priest for each of the three sections.

The ritual should be conducted once a month if possible, on any day agreed by the group. Whenever this day falls near a date that is especially holy to any member of the group, the ritual consists of all four parts described below. When the ritual does not occur near a holy day, it includes only the first three parts. Serve enough food and drink for a feast on a full holy day, and enough for a snack at other times.

Preparations: Place incense or a candle, matches, an offering plate and cup, and a plate of food or a full meal in the area of worship.

1- Blessing

The group gathers in a circle.

The priest lights incense or a candle and walks sunwise around the group to bless them and create sacred space, then sets the candle or incense down in an appropriate place.

The priest speaks an opening blessing in honor of the elemental powers or nature spirits.

Going sunwise around the circle, each member who wishes to may offer a prayer in honor of the elemental powers or nature spirits.

2- Ancestor Veneration

The priest speaks a blessing for the dead and asks their blessing on the group.

Going sunwise around the circle, each member who wishes to may offer a prayer to the dead or ancestors.

3- Offering

The priest makes an offering of food and drink to the gods, the ancestors, and the powers of nature. The priest invites the powers to share food and drink with the group.

Going sunwise around the circle, each member who wishes to may offer a prayer to any gods they worship. Prayer can continue in as many rounds as needed until everyone is done.

Sharing of food and drink.

4- Celebration

Music, dance and celebration. This portion of the ritual is informal and celebratory, and may involve ecstatic dance, or trance states. Any members with a question to ask may request divination services at this time if a diviner is present.

APPENDIX 2: SOURCES AND FURTHER READING

WHAT IS PAGAN ANARCHISM?

Wilby, Emma. **The Visions of Isobel Gowdie Magic: *Witchcraft and Dark Shamanism in Seventeenth-Century Scotland*.** Sussex Academic Press, 2011

Marshall, Peter. **Demanding the Impossible: *A History of Anarchism*.** PM Press, 2008

A SHORT HISTORY OF PAGANISM

Grey, Peter. **Apocalyptic Witchcraft.** Scarlet Imprint, 2013

Hutton, Ronald. **The Pagan Religions of the Ancient British Isles: *Their Nature and Legacy*.** Blackwell Publishing, 1993

Cohn, Norman. **The Pursuit of the Millennium: *Revolutionary Millenarians and Mystical Anarchists of the Middle Ages*.** Oxford University Press, 1970

Federici, Silvia. **Caliban and the Witch: *Women, the Body and Primitive Accumulation*.** Autonomedia, 2004

Hanegraff, Wouter. **New Age Religion and Western Culture: *Esotericism in the Mirror of Secular Thought*.** Brill Academic Publishers, 1996

Leland, Charles Godfrey. **Aradia.** 1899

Wilby, Emma. **The Visions of Isobel Gowdie: *Magic, Witchcraft and Dark Shamanism in Seventeenth-Century Scotland*.** Sussex Academic Press, 2011

CHRISTOPHER SCOTT THOMPSON

THE STORY OF AN IDEA

Scott, James C. **The Art of Not Being Governed:** *An Anarchist History of Upland Southeast Asia.* Yale University Press, 2009

Godwin, William. **An Enquiry Concerning the Principles of Political Justice and Its Influence on General Virtue and Happiness.** 1793

Oswald, John. **The Cry of Nature, or An Appeal to Mercy and Justice, on Behalf of the Persecuted Animals.** 1791

Proudhon, P.J. **What is Property:** *An Inquiry into the Principle of Right and Government.* 1840

Proudhon, P.J. **The General Idea of the Revolution.** 1851

Stirner, Max. **The Ego and Its Own.** 1845

Bakunin, Mikhail. **Letters to A Frenchman on the Present Crisis.** 1870

Bakunin, Mikhail. **God and the State.** 1882

Kropotkin, Peter. **The Conquest of Bread.** 1892

Kropotkin, Peter. **Mutual Aid:** *A Factor of Evolution.* 1902

MacGregor-Reid, George Watson. **The Natural Basis of Civilization.** 1893

Linebaugh, Peter. **The Incomplete, True, Authentic & Wonderful History of May Day.** PM Press, 2016

Goldman, Emma. **Anarchism and Other Essays.** 1910

De Cleyre, Voltairine. **The Voltairine de Cleyre Reader.** AK Press, 2004

Starhawk. **The Spiral Dance:** *A Rebirth of the Ancient Religion of the Great Goddess.* Harper and Row, 1979

White, Roger. **Post Colonial Anarchism:** *Essays on Race, Repression and Culture in Communities of Color.* Jailbreak Press

Ervin, Lorenzo Kom'boa. **Anarchism and the Black Revolution.** 1993

Various. **Queering Anarchism:** *Addressing and Undressing Power and Desire.* AK Press, 2012

Zerzan, John (editor). **Against Civilization:** *Readings and Reflections.* 2005

Bookchin, Murray. **Post-Scarcity Anarchism.** Ramparts Press, 1971

Bookchin, Murray. **The Ecology of Freedom:** *The Emergence and Dissolution of Hierarchy.* Cheshire Books, 1982

BRINGING THE MAGIC BACK

Weber, Max. **The Protestant Ethic and the Spirit of Capitalism.** 1905

Weber, Max. **Science as a Vocation.** 1917

Federici, Silvia. **Caliban and the Witch:** *Women, the Body and Primitive Accumulation.* Autonomedia, 2004

BONFIRES AND REVELRY

Moore, John. "**A Primitivist Primer,**" originally published in Green Anarchist magazine

"**To Rust Metallic Gods:** *An Anarcho-Primitivist Critique of Paganism.*" published in Black and Green Review, Issue 1

Killjoy, Margaret. "**Take What You Need and Compost the Rest:** *An Introduction to Post-Civilized Theory.*" The Anarchist Library (theanarchistlibrary.org), 2010

Zerzan, John (editor). **Against Civilization:** *Readings and Reflections.* 2005

Hickel, Jason. **"Clean Energy Won't Save Us - Only a New Economic System Can,"** on the Guardian (theguardian.com)

IN THE NAME OF THE UNDEAD

Lecouteux, Claude. **The Return of the Dead:** *Ghosts, Ancestors, and the Transparent Veil of the Pagan Mind.* Inner Traditions, 2009

Heathen Chinese. "**Millenarianism Pt.2, The Yellow Turbans.**" Heathen Chinese: Diasporic Chinese Polytheism (heathenchinese.wordpress.com)

A CITY WHERE GODS CAN LIVE

Bookchin, Murray. **Post-Scarcity Anarchism.** Ramparts Press, 1971

Bookchin, Murray. **The Ecology of Freedom:** *The Emergence and Dissolution of Hierarchy.* Cheshire Books, 1982

Öcalan, Abdullah. **Democratic Confederalism.** Transmedia Publishing, 2011

Anderson, Tom. "**Democratic Confederalism in Kurdistan.**" Corporate Watch (corporatewatch.org)

CHRISTOPHER SCOTT THOMPSON

Watson, David. **Beyond Bookchin:** *Preface for a Future Social Ecology, Black &* *Red.* Autonomedia, 1996

MY FAMILIAR IS SABOCAT!

Hardy, Ernest George. **Christianity and the Roman Government:** *A Study in* *Imperial Administration.* 1894

x344543. **"The Black Cat (Sabo-Tabby)."** IWW website (IWW.org)

X344543. **"Direct Action and Sabotage."** IWW website (IWW.org)

Wainwright, Oliver. "**In Iceland, Respect the Elves, Or Else.**" The Guardian (theguardian.com)

Coulter, Peter. **"Fairy Tales:** *Finding Fairy Bushes Across Northern Ireland."* on BBC News (bbc.co.uk)

Leland, Charles Godfrey. **Aradia.** 1899

Dr. Bones, "**Folk-Magic as Insurrection.**" Gods & Radicals (godsandradicals.org)

Grey, Peter. **Apocalyptic Witchcraft.** Scarlet Imprint, 2013

Skuggi. **The Sorcerer's Screed.** Lesstofan, 2015

Summers, Montague. **Witchcraft and Black Magic.** Dover Publications, 2012

MANY GODS, NO MASTERS

Sheppard, Brian Oliver. **Anarchism vs. Primitivism.** The Anarchist Library (theanarchistlibrary.org)

ABOUT THE AUTHOR

Christopher Scott Thompson became a pagan at age 12, inspired by books of mythology and the experience of homesteading in rural Maine. A devotee of the Celtic goddesses Brighid and Macha, Thompson has been active in the pagan and polytheist communities as an author, activist and founding member of Clann Bhride (The Children of Brighid). Thompson was active in Occupy Minnesota and is currently a member of the Workers' Solidarity Alliance, an anarcho-syndicalist organization. He is also the founder of the Cateran Society, an organization that studies the historical martial art of the Highland broadsword. Thompson lives with his family in Portland, Maine.

GODS&RADICALS

Founded on Beltane, 2015, Gods&Radicals is a non-profit, Pagan Anti-Capitalist Publisher and a site of Beautiful Resistance. For more information or to find our other works, please contact us at

Editor@godsandradicals.org,

or visit

GodsAndRadicals.org

CPSIA information can be obtained
at www.ICGtesting.com
Printed in the USA
LVHW010143290720
661635LV00002B/212